HOLD THE LINE

My Story from the Heart of the Freedom Convoy

TAMARA LICH

About Rebel News

Rebel News is Canada's largest independent source of news, opinion and activism. Because Rebel News takes no money from any government, it is able to report candidly on controversial events, like the trucker convoy. Rebel News's motto is "telling the other side of the story" — in Canada and across the world.

For more information about Rebel News, or more copies of this book, please visit *www.RebelNews.com*

REBELNEWS

TELLING THE OTHER SIDE OF THE STORY

TABLE OF CONTENTS

ACKNOWLEDGMENTS

I'd like to thank my husband Dwayne for his support and Rupa Subramanya for her beautiful foreword. Thanks also to Ben Stanley for his editorial assistance and to Rebel News for publishing the book.

And none of this would have been possible without the love and support from millions of Canadians. They inspired me and they inspired the world.

FOREWORD
BY RUPA SUBRAMANYA

When the Freedom Convoy rolled into Ottawa on January 28, 2022, little did I know that this protest movement would become a pivotal cultural moment in modern Canadian history. The political establishment, including Prime Minister Justin Trudeau and his echo chamber in the legacy media, had been tarring members of the convoy as far right extremists, racists, misogynists -- the list goes on. When I heard these over-the-top attempts to smear the protesters, I knew something was not right. I'd seen this tactic used by the establishment in other countries to vilify those outside the establishment.

I walked around from morning till evening everyday in the bitter cold for three weeks. There were times when the temperature dropped down to -30 and an extreme cold warning was issued. Why would anyone want to protest in such conditions, and what does it tell us about the character of the people protesting? Many of the truckers were away from family and friends. Many had lost their jobs. They were using up their limited savings to sit in their trucks in the freezing cold. This told me in no uncertain terms that they were sincere, dedicated and determined to put their views across, and to do so peacefully in the nation's capital.

The gathering felt more like a winter carnival, almost like Canada Day in January. There were Canadian flags everywhere. Everyone there believed fervently that there was a Canadian identity to be cherished and protected. They didn't believe Trudeau, when he claimed a few years back that Canada was now a "post-national" state, and therefore had no cultural identity. Trudeau had gone so far as to lower the national flag on Parliament Hill for months on end, in an act of national self-flagellation for the the supposed sins of the past. For Trudeau, as for the woke progressive elite, Canada was a racist and colonial settler state. The Freedom Convoy protesters from all parts of the country -- and from every conceivable ethnicity -- were there to reclaim the flag and assert that Canada was a country worth fighting for.

I got to know many of the protesters over the three weeks or so that the Freedom Convoy was in Ottawa, until it was brutally suppressed by Trudeau's use of draconian emergency powers. I came to know some of the organizers of the protest, notably Tamara Lich, who became one of the key faces and voices of the protest. It was hard not to like Tamara. She was warm and engaging, yet feisty and tough as nails, and wasn't going to back down in the face of intimidation from the powers that be. She knew from the first day that she herself and other organizers might be arrested, yet this did not deter her in a just cause.

That was the message that came through loud and clear from all the protesters I spoke to. They weren't in Ottawa just to fight for themselves, but to reveal the fundamental injustice of the government's approach to the pandemic, especially the harsh vaccine mandates. They wanted to work toward a fairer and more just Canada, that would take different and sincerely held opinions into account, and not try to ride roughshod over the individual liberties of Canadians.

Contrary to the official narrative that the protesters were "anti-science", many protesters I met had a strong understanding of science and the scientific method. Some of them were doctors and nurses who had been laid off for not complying with the mandates. They were educators, accountants, civil servants, writers and artists and of course truckers. They spanned the spectrum of every profession and walk of life. They objected to government mandates that would force people who had legitimate concerns about a rapidly developed and largely untested new vaccine. There was a shared conviction that it was a matter of principle to stand up against divide-and-rule policies, that were not only dividing the country but tearing families apart.

My friend, the civil servant from Ottawa, told me when we first met on a frigid day at the protests, that he was standing up against the mandates, not for himself, but for many of his fellow Canadians. He was fighting the good fight for future generations so they didn't have to be part of something unjust that created more divisions in society. As he put it, "As a public servant, I refused to help the government create a second class citizenry". He knew going against the grain would cost him his job and his livelihood. He was one of 1,200 federal civil servants who were placed on leave without pay for not complying with the mandate, in a service comprising of more than 300,000 employees. It would mean that some friends and family might stop speaking to him. And that's exactly what happened yet none of that deterred him.

This courage was contagious. There was a powerful sense of awakening, as people began to reclaim their lives and that of their fellow Canadians from capricious, opportunistic, and unprincipled government policy. The Freedom Convoy and the truckers sitting in their trucks blaring their horns were giving voice to the voiceless. Those who had been ignored would be ignored no longer. To some of the protesters I spoke to, the horns sounding were like the trumpets of angels heralding a new beginning or so it felt last winter in Ottawa. As my friend put it to me: "I didn't expect God to send angels in trucks."

The awakening was something new. In the modern history of Canada, since the Second World War, there had never been a protest of this kind -- that was standing up for our right to choose and pushing back against government overreach in our private lives. So powerful was the message, it struck a chord not just in Canada but around the world, with similar protests being organized in places as far flung as New Zealand, Belgium, and Argentina. The protests in Ottawa lit a candle for freedom which illumined much of the world. People who had become used to living under government diktat for almost two years woke up to the fact that governments everywhere had encroached on their civil liberties. It was time to push back against an ever expanding state machinery.

Tamara exemplified this new Canadian spirit. She paid a price for standing up for our fundamental rights and freedoms. Intimidated and harassed by the authorities after the Freedom Convoy was broken up, she spent time in jail waiting for bail, facing treatment meted out by the criminal justice system that was far harsher than that faced by to heinous criminals. The system clearly wanted to make an example out of her. But even in the face of such oppression, she has continued to be courageous and graceful under pressure and keeps fighting the good fight.

In this book, Tamara shares her journey with all of us. Future generations will look back on the Freedom Convoy and its leaders, especially Tamara, for keeping ideals over expediency, and always holding the line.

CHAPTER 1:

'I AM SOMEBODY ELSE'

Consider it officially confirmed — by me: If you're a visible minority who stands for a government-approved left-wing cause, you're celebrated as a hero. If you're an Aboriginal leader fighting against oil and gas, the CBC will assign teams of reporters to lionize your struggle on the evening news. But you'll be treated a lot differently if you're a Metis grandma with the wrong politics.

Just a few weeks after the Freedom Convoy, the CBC ran a segment on *The National* called "Using Indigenous knowledge to tackle climate change."[1] It checked all their favourite boxes. They even have a whole news department, called CBC Indigenous, that's wall-to-wall coverage about Aboriginal activists — who all happen to fit with the CBC's view of what Aboriginal activists should be doing: denouncing colonialism[2],

1 https://www.youtube.com/watch?v=SjSzx0_7yPY

2 https://www.cbc.ca/news/canada/british-columbia/indigenous-communities-bc-monarchy-reconciliation-queens-death-1.6578284

opposing industrial projects[3], demanding "climate action"[4], banning glyphosate[5] or whatever.

It's not just the CBC, either; most of the mainstream media seems to think the best use of what few resources they still have is spent scouring the country (or, more often, Twitter) for stories about "BIPOC" people[6] agitating for left-wing causes, whether it's climate, anti-racism, feminism, trans rights, or anti-capitalism.

But things tend to change when you're fighting for something the CBC, the mainstream media and the government don't like.

In all the hundreds of news stories that covered the Freedom Convoy, portraying me as the "leader," almost none mentioned my Aboriginal heritage.

And the few times it came up, it sure wasn't celebrated. It was scrutinized, doubted and questioned.

My grandmother was a Cree. My grandfather was a Cree. My birth mother, who came from a family of 13 children, put me up for adoption in Saskatoon, Saskatchewan, and I was adopted at two months old. I know it wasn't easy for her. Even though my grandparents had very much wanted her to keep me so they could raise me, she just thought it would be better for me to be in a stable home with two parents, and that I'd have a better chance at life. I was adopted by Stan McBurney, who comes from Irish roots, and Bonnie, who comes from Norwegian roots. And I was blessed to be born and raised in Saskatchewan. Actually, I stayed all over Saskatchewan.

---

3 https://www.cbc.ca/news/canada/north/yukon-chilkat-valley-watershed-klukwan-1.6576319

4 https://www.cbc.ca/news/indigenous/kahnawake-youth-cop26-delegates-1.6226017

5 https://www.cbc.ca/documentaries/the-passionate-eye/a-group-of-first-nations-elders-is-trying-to-ban-glyphosate-they-say-it-s-killing-their-way-of-life-1.6497383

6 "BIPOC" is the woke acronym for Black, Indigenous and People of Colour.

I was lucky in other ways, too. When my parents first married, my mom had three miscarriages. After the last one, the doctor told her the sad news that it was possible she would never have children. And so I became a McBurney — and then, what do you know?, they had five more children. I have two brothers and three sisters, and I grew up in a big, loving family. Naturally, we fought a lot. And it was chaos sometimes. But mom and dad kept us busy enough that we didn't have enough time to do too much damage.

We also moved around — a lot. My dad was a buyer for the Saskatchewan Wheat Pool when I was young and then moved into the oil and gas sector. My parents are sort of like gypsies. My dad can't seem to sit still for long and I believe I get my rolling spirit from him. Moving around doesn't let your roots grow very deep but it teaches you to become adaptable. Even today, he and my mom work driving pilot trucks — going on long trips, driving ahead of the big rigs hauling wide loads, to make sure the way is cleared for the wide loads to pass through.

Growing up, we lived in a lot of places in Saskatchewan that most Canadians have probably never heard of: Coronach, Horizon, Alida, Shaunavon, Eastend, Dollard, Simmie. I think I went to six or seven different schools growing up. My favourite places were in the country, when we lived on farms, which was the case a couple of times. The country is where I love to be. I adored riding horses; I used to ride every day, and I always went along on the round-ups and trail rides.

In Grade 9 we moved to Frontier, Sask. where I would attend high school. They must have named it Frontier because there's exactly what it is. It's as flat and bald as you can get in Saskatchewan, primarily farm and grasslands. My parents ended up owning the Frontier Inn, a motel and restaurant on the edge of town. I worked there, as did most of my siblings — bussing tables, waiting, doing dishes, cooking, you name it.

I moved to Shaunavon, Sask. after Grade 12, renting a little house with my best friend from elementary school and my first daughter who was born in the spring of 1990. (I would eventually have two more daughters.) I was there to attend the first semester at Shaunavon High in order to complete the high-school credits that I needed to graduate. From there I moved around other parts of Saskatchewan, to Moose Jaw, then back to Frontier, then back to Shaunavon — and then to Medicine Hat, Alta., which is where I live now. I guess, like my parents, I have trouble sitting still.

But my parents were always open about my adoption, and ensured that I knew my heritage, both Scottish and Métis. Although I met my biological mother for the first time when I was in my late teens (she lives in Alberta) as far back as I can remember I've felt strong connection to my Indigenous heritage. There weren't a lot of Indigenous people in Shaunavon or Frontier so any learning about my heritage, I had to go and do on my own. Around 2008, I remember travelling through Manitoba to a weekend of self discovery near Hillside Beach at Ma Mawi Wi Chi Itata Centre, a 'Training, Healing and Learning' facility whose website says, "We all work together to help one another" and whose mandate states "We are a community of people helping other community people reclaim our inherent roles and responsibilities as Indigenous caregivers and the most important teachers of our children." Here, I met a beautiful family who had agreed to let me attend and to work with me over the course of the weekend even though they didn't normally do retreats with only a single participant. I understood and appreciated how lucky I was to have that opportunity.

I was introduced to many Indigenous concepts, was able to attend a sweat lodge ceremony and learned about the medicine wheel. Since meeting my mother and her family, I've gotten to learn more about my birth family and my ancestry. One aunt has given me tons of photos of my birth family, which have meant so much to me, and regularly posts old family photos on her social media. My adopted family and I were quite a close family when we were young, yet I was always aware growing up that I didn't look like anybody in my family. That might sound strange. But it was a big deal to me. I often wondered or thought "I must look like somebody, somewhere." When my aunt showed me pictures of my birth mother when she was younger I remember a few uncontrollable tears rolling down my cheeks. I looked like someone! In fact, I looked exactly like someone. I had found a piece of what made me, me.

But being a person with Native blood who stands for things that aren't part of the mainstream media and Liberal party's agenda, of course means that the first thing the media will do is try to prove you're not actually of Native blood. After all, they figure anyone with an Indigenous background must think alike, right? They're all against pipelines, and oil sands, and they all want more government support. Remember when Justin Trudeau condescended to Native chiefs[7], by telling them that what Native kids really need is "a place to store their canoes and paddles so they can connect back out on the land," and not the youth centres the chiefs wanted? Places where on-reserve kids could have a safe place to hang out? The only Aboriginal people that Trudeau has any interest in are the stereotypes. And whatever I am, one thing I know for sure: I'm no stereotype.

That meant that as soon as I became identified with the Freedom Convoy, the first job of the Trudeau fan-club media was to try to prove that I'm not actually Aboriginal. After I was arrested, I presented to the court my membership card from the Alberta Métis Nation. And the government-funded Aboriginal Peoples Television Network ran a story that "Genealogist says more information needed on whether Tamara Lich is Métis." They actually went and found a genealogist so they could put my ancestry on trial, in the media. And the only thing this genealogist, Gail Morin, could tell them was that she didn't know one way or the other. "Morin said she wouldn't be able to confirm Lich is Métis without knowing the name of her grandparents." What a scoop, APTN. They found someone who didn't know anything about my ancestry to say they didn't know anything about my ancestry. All

7 https://nationalpost.com/news/politics/john-ivison-trudeau-was-always-a-joke-to-the-right-he-should-worry-now-the-lefts-joined-in-the-laughter

so they could run a story that not-so-subtly implied that I might be lying about my ancestry.

The Ottawa Citizen[8] said about me that Lich "claims Métis heritage." Global News[9] said only that I "described myself as Metis." Even though I have a membership card in the Alberta Metis Nation. And even the Wikipedia entry about me[10] says dubiously that I have "publicly claimed Métis heritage." Do you think they do that for other Native people? Do they qualify their identity by saying they "publicly claim" Native heritage? You can go ahead and have a look for yourself: They don't.

Meanwhile, other reporters[11] found Métis and Aboriginal leaders to denounce both me and other Métis and Aboriginal people who participated in the Freedom Convoy. Because the Indigenous people I saw in Ottawa didn't fit the Liberal stereotype either — but they sure were 100-per-cent authentic, freedom-loving Indigenous people. So we were condemned for the teepees, the pipe ceremonies and the Métis flags that had been set up in Ottawa: "these individuals and this convoy in no way represent what we believe in," said one Manitoba Métis leader. I don't recall these people speaking out when some of these same symbols were used during rail blockades[12] and anti-oil protests[13].

Actually, up until the last few years, I wasn't really the sort of person who publicly protests. But there's something about living under Justin

8 https://ottawacitizen.com/news/local-news/who-is-tamara-lich-the-spark-that-lit-the-fire

9 https://globalnews.ca/news/8978193/convoy-tamara-lich-freedom-mandate-metis/

10 https://en.wikipedia.org/wiki/Tamara_Lich

11 https://winnipeg.ctvnews.ca/manitoba-métis-federation-condemns-use-ofmétis-symbols-in-anti-restriction-convoys-1.5768391

12 https://warriorpublications.wordpress.com/2013/01/03/idle-no-more-protesters-block-eastern-quebec-rail-line/

13 https://www.cbc.ca/news/canada/new-brunswick/teepee-unites-anti-fracking-protesters-1.988678

Trudeau's Liberal government that seems to have turned a lot of people into the sort who publicly protest. It seems that having a government that represents less than one-third of the Canadian population, and spends all its time attacking the Canadians that don't support it, will do that to a country.

When I was growing up, my parents were not the skeptical sort. They taught me all about the importance of honesty, integrity and trust. Maybe I have come to be a little too trusting sometimes. They were always the kind of people that took strangers into their homes and cooked them a meal, or if they were stuck on the highway, they'd bring them home or give them money. They were always helping other people. We woke up many times with strangers on our couch. And I think that's one of the most important things they taught me is the value of taking care of people and always helping them to be in a better place when you leave them than they were when you found them. And everyone they took in was grateful for it. I don't think they were ever betrayed by someone stealing from them or hurting them. They were very good, trusting people. And they still are today.

So maybe I was just too trusting, for too long, assuming people were generally good, and our leaders had our country's best interests at heart. Up until the early 2000s, I wasn't very political at all. It was through my former husband's influence that I began reading the *National Post,* following current events and loosely following Canadian politics. I began to follow considerably more closely however around 2004 and the breaking of the Liberal sponsorship scandal and my eyes began to open as I realized how shady politics could be. And as I started watching bits of question period and political conversations on television, I started to become increasingly fascinated — and frustrated.

Take question period, for example, where the government is supposed to be made to answer for the decisions it makes. But as the old joke goes, it's not called answer period, and it's true: they simply don't answer the questions they don't want to. I started to realize there is no accountability there. I'd seen more maturity and transparency in a kindergarten class and this is what they were serving up to the Canadian people?! But what could I do about it? Like so many Canadians who see a system that doesn't work for the people, but instead is designed to work for the politicians, I would just throw up my hands, or shake my head and turn the channel. There were obviously things at stake that were going to affect me at least in some indirect way, but it didn't seem like I could do anything to stop it, except to wait for the next election to roll around. Even then, being in Alberta meant that voters here had little power. Our federal elections are essentially decided by Ontario and, especially, Quebec, and our leaders always make sure those provinces come first. The sponsorship scandal that first woke me up to the reality of how politics is usually done in this country was all about the federal Liberal government sloshing tons of money around to keep Quebec happy to stop the separatist threat (while skimming off some money for the Liberal party itself). Of course the Liberals wanted to keep Quebec from separating: Without Quebec, they wouldn't be as politically powerful. And no wonder they don't seem to care about making Alberta unhappy: if Alberta were to separate, it would only make it even less likely for Conservatives to win power.

Living in Alberta, I've worked most of my career in the oil and gas industry. It was when I was working at the global energy services company Schlumberger that I discovered that I was really, really good at managing logistics and better yet, I loved it! It's a skill that would come in very handy in my life.

I started at Schlumberger working 12-hour shifts as a dispatcher for the crews who provide cementing and acid services on wellsites. Working a night shift meant there were often quiet periods, most notably throughout spring break up. I became good friends with my counterparts at our Red Deer base who worked in frac logistics, a more complicated logistics process, who took the time to teach me about the fracturing process, the hows and the whys. It had way more moving parts and it was fascinating to me; from equipment and manpower needs for each job to understanding why certain chemicals were used and when.

It was the early 2000s, during one of Alberta's occasional oil and gas booms, and people were drilling all over the place. Our Medicine Hat base became busy enough that they made the decision to move Medicine Hat dispatching to our base. Up until then everything had been organized out of Red Deer. I was offered the frac logistics position and jumped at the opportunity. I enjoyed the fast pace, found that I could work well under pressure and with imminent deadlines. While most jobs were similar, they were all unique and I loved the challenging aspects as well as the many different inputs: the sand they inject underground to loosen the gas from the shale, the chemicals, and all the equipment. In Alberta during booms, there are always issues with making sure you have enough manpower. I was juggling all of these different things that needed to be picked up, delivered or borrowed from other Schlumberger bases in the province and was fortunate to work under the direction and guidance of some really great managers. I was learning how to organize complicated operations. When the Freedom Convoy happened, these skills were a huge help.

Working in the oil and gas sector has meant that I've seen firsthand the damage that the anti-oil agenda of the Trudeau Liberals is doing to our economy and, more importantly, to people's lives. Alberta's always had its booms and busts, of course. That's something we've always accepted as part of the deal. We thrive by the market and we die by the market, and that's fair. That's freedom.

But when Justin Trudeau was elected prime minister, he decided Alberta simply wasn't going to thrive — period. His principal secretary, best friend, and the guy who made all his decisions for him was Gerald Butts, who comes from the radical anti-fossil-fuel movement. Previously in his career, Butts was behind the disastrous "green energy" policies of former Ontario premier Dalton McGuinty that destroyed that province's electric system and forced Ontarians[14] to choose between paying their skyrocketing hydro bills and eating. That was before Butts went to work as CEO for the World Wildlife Fund, which has been trying to shut down Alberta's oilsands[15]. He left the WWF, after Trudeau was elected, to work in the Prime Minister's Office, so he could shut in Alberta oil using the power of the federal government. But then Butts was also instrumental in the dirty SNC Lavalin scandal and the even dirtier WE Charity scandal, so I'm not surprised that he seems to lack enough of a moral compass to realize how his anti-oil militancy is hurting hundreds of thousands of people, while making zero difference to the climate.

Unlike Butts and Trudeau and Catherine McKenna, their former environment minister, I think Canadian governments should serve our people, not the UN and its Intergovernmental Panel on Climate Change. I think that if laws are passed that hurt more Canadians than they help, then those are obviously bad laws. And it was two of those bad laws — Bill C-48 and Bill C-69 — that finally made me realize that I couldn't throw up my hands and shake my head at Ottawa anymore. I had to take a stand.

Bill C-48 and Bill C-69 are two laws that are incredibly unfair to Alberta. They were passed right when Alberta was facing a recession and rising unemployment. Bill C-48 made it illegal for tankers to take Alberta crude oil from the north of B.C.'s coast. That makes it impossible for Alberta to get its crude to overseas markets by building a pipeline like Northern Gateway, which the Liberals have also refused to allow. It's basically Ottawa telling Alberta that we can't sell our oil overseas. The only pipeline allowed from Alberta to the coast is the Trans Mountain pipeline, which mostly feeds refineries and fuel consumption in the Pacific Northwest, and can't keep up with demand

14 https://globalnews.ca/news/3179769/justin-trudeau-confronted-by-sobbing-ontario-woman-over-cost-of-hydro-bill/

15 https://c2cjournal.ca/2019/03/killing-the-tar-sands-with-american-money-and-canadian-saboteurs/

as it is. (The Trans Mountain expansion, if it ever happens, is supposed to help with that, but I'm sure Steven Guilbeault, the Greenpeace activist now serving as federal environment minister, is already working on ways to ban any possibility of that.)

And Bill C-69 was even worse. They called it the "no more pipelines" bill. The bill, officially called the Impact Assessment Act, basically makes it impossible for any oil and gas project to ever get built again by dramatically raising the thresholds one would have to meet to get federal approval. It used to be that to get an energy project approved, proponents would have to satisfy an environmental impact assessment. That was difficult enough: Canada already has some of the most stringent environmental protections in the world, where investors in an energy project would have to show that they wouldn't do any serious damage the ecosystem, wildlife, air quality and so on, and would need to have a plan to remediate whatever disruptions they caused. That wasn't good enough for Trudeau and McKenna. To be more precise, it wasn't good enough because energy investors kept meeting the stringent environmental impact conditions, and so regulators continued to approve oil and gas projects.

Trudeau and McKenna apparently didn't want oil and gas projects to be approved. They wanted them shut down. They radically expanded the scope of the approval process to make approvals much more difficult.

One of the most bizarre new Liberal-imposed assessments for a new energy project would be its "social impacts." If you're wondering what kind of social impact an underground pipeline has, don't even try to figure it out: it doesn't. But the law was basically a way for the Trudeau Liberals to take approvals out of the hands of traditionally neutral regulators and let politicians decide what gets built and what doesn't. They even made it so that projects would have to undergo "gender-based analysis."

It was such an overreach into constitutionally protected provincial sovereignty over resources that even Quebec opposed it[16] (and the Quebec government is totally hostile to Alberta oil, which Quebec Premier Francois Legault calls "dirty energy"). In May 2022, the Alberta Court of Appeal ruled the bill was unconstitutional. It said the Constitution was clear that "where an activity, such as an intra-provincial designated project, is otherwise within exclusive provincial jurisdiction, Parliament's jurisdiction is limited to the environmental effects of that activity." In other words, the system we had before Trudeau and McKenna dreamed up their crazy Bill C-69. Naturally, the Liberals have refused to repeal the law and say they'll fight the ruling — and Alberta's right to use its resources — all the way to the Supreme Court.

Remember, these were just the most explicit, naked attacks on Alberta's industry, the ones where the Trudeau Liberals didn't even put much effort into disguising what they were trying to do. But they were hardly the only attacks. Since being elected, Trudeau had talked about "phasing out"[17] the oilsands. He outright vetoed plans for the Northern Gateway pipeline that would have taken oil from Alberta to northern British Columbia, despite the fact that most Aboriginal communities in B.C.'s north supported[18] the pipeline.

Another pipeline, Energy East, was supposed to be a nation-building project that would take raw bitumen from Alberta's oilsands to be upgraded in refineries in Eastern Canada. Provinces east of Manitoba actually import a lot of their oil from overseas[19], and from

---

16 https://www.theglobeandmail.com/opinion/article-what-national-unity-crisis-even-quebec-thinks-c-69-is-a-bad-bill/

17 https://calgaryherald.com/news/politics/we-need-to-phase-them-out-trudeau-draws-fire-over-oilsands-remark

18 https://financialpost.com/commodities/energy/we-are-very-disappointed-loss-of-northern-gateway-devastating-for-many-first-nations-chiefs-say

19 https://www.cer-rec.gc.ca/en/data-analysis/energy-commodities/crude-oil-petroleum-products/report/archive/2019-gasoline/index.html

places where production[20] is far less ethical, or environmentally friendly, than in Alberta, including Saudi Arabia, Azerbaijan, Iraq, Nigeria, Colombia, Kazakhstan, Algeria and Russia. So Energy East would have let Canadians use Canadian oil, instead of conflict oil, while creating thousands of jobs across the country. It would also allow Alberta to trade its oil for the same market value that Eastern Canadians were paying for imported oil, rather than having to take a discount by sending it through overloaded pipelines in the U.S. At times, that discount has been as much as US$50 a barrel, robbing Albertans of billions of dollars' worth of value every year, while Americans buy our exports on the cheap.

But Quebecers said they didn't want a pipeline carrying Alberta oil running across their province. And Trudeau announced that the pipeline would have to meet a whole new set of impossible reviews before his government would approve it, including not just how many carbon emissions the pipeline would create, which wouldn't be that much, but all the carbon emissions that would result from consumers using the oil shipped in the pipeline. The Liberals had come up with yet another entirely new assessment[21]. It was an ambush.

The end uses of oil are the same whether the oil is shipped by train or by pipeline. But that wasn't the point. TransCanada, the company behind the pipeline, saw the writing on the wall. There was no way the Trudeau Liberals would approve a pipeline if it would cost them votes in Quebec. TransCanada cancelled Energy East.

And then there's the gift that keeps on giving: Trudeau's carbon tax. The tax started at $20 per tonne in 2019 and it's already up to $50 in 2022. Even though oil and gas prices were already way up due to soaring demand in 2022, with economies coming out of lockdown and

20 https://www.cer-rec.gc.ca/en/data-analysis/energy-markets/market-snapshots/2022/market-snapshot-crude-oil-imports-declined-in-2021-while-refined-petroleum-product-imports-rose-modestly.html

21 https://nationalpost.com/news/politics/john-ivison-trudeaus-liberals-have-kept-all-the-pipeline-promises-they-intended-to-keep

supply problems from Russia's invasion of Ukraine, the Liberals went ahead and raised the tax even more, as if Canadians weren't having enough trouble being able to afford to fill up their tanks and heat their homes. And it's become pretty clear that, of all the provinces, the tax hits Alberta the hardest: A recent study from the Fraser Institute[22] found that the carbon tax will cause Alberta's economy to shrink more than the national average and lose more than 30,000 jobs.

When I was growing up in Saskatchewan, it was very much a have-not province. And we always heard the tales how great and prosperous Alberta was. There was a province that not only had a lot of resources, but it was the Wild West — in a good way. Investors were welcome, producers were free to pump oil, taxes were kept low, and the whole province was better off for it. It was the land of opportunity. It even had a name: "The Alberta Advantage." Millions of people flocked to Alberta, including from Saskatchewan. In the years before Trudeau was elected, Statistics Canada was even showing data projecting that Alberta's population would probably overtake that of British Columbia by 2038 — just over 15 years from now — and that it might, a few decades out, have more people than even Quebec[23], and become Canada's second-largest province (Alberta's economy is already nearly as big as Quebec's, with half as many people). I can imagine how that would throw Liberals into a panic. They can't let Alberta become that powerful, especially relative to Quebec, the province from which the Liberals get much of their power. The whole climate change thing that Trudeau uses to justify his anti-oil legislation is just a pretext: Alberta actually produces some of the cleanest energy in the world. After all, the Liberals just recently approved[24] the controversial Bay

22 https://www.fraserinstitute.org/article/new-170-carbon-tax-will-hit-albertans-hard

23 https://www.macleans.ca/economy/economicanalysis/could-alberta-pass-quebec-to-become-the-second-largest-province/

24 https://www.cbc.ca/news/canada/newfoundland-labrador/bay-du-nord-approval-1.6410509

du Nord offshore-oil megaproject in Newfoundland, outraging his climate crusading friends. (Atlantic Canada is another region where the Liberals are popular). Trudeau isn't trying to stop oil production, or oil consumption for that matter. Just over the last year or so, Trudeau himself has burned enough fuel[25] in his plane to fly around the entire Earth three times. He just wants to stick it to Alberta.

Unfortunately, it seems to be working. I think Alberta is in trouble. Tens of billions of dollars of investment have been scrapped because Trudeau has made it clear he'll block anyone who wants to develop Alberta's resources. Shell has sold off its Alberta assets. So has Norway's Statoil. Encana, an Alberta-born success story, relocated to the United States.

I'm not sure there's even an Alberta Advantage anymore that makes it better to live here than anywhere else in the country. That doesn't mean Alberta can't be great again. It just means we're going to have to stop Liberal politicians from being able to attack us.

With all this happening, I found myself starting getting fed up and pushing back for the first time against Ottawa and Trudeau's government before the pandemic started. When the Liberals began attacking Alberta, I had to do something, even if I didn't yet know exactly what. As the Liberals announced more and more laws attacking Alberta and the oil and gas industry, I started joining rallies for the Yellow Vest Movement in Canada. The movement was inspired by the "Mouvement des gilets jaunes" (the same name in French) that had been happening in France in 2018 after the government there had begun imposing increasingly heavy carbon taxes[26] and was about to raise taxes again on diesel fuel, which of course is used by truck and equipment drivers, a.k.a. working-class people. This, while French

25 https://nationalpost.com/news/politics/trudeau-burns-the-jet-fuel-flying-equivalent-of-three-trips-around-the-earth-over-past-10-months

26 https://theconversation.com/emmanuel-macrons-carbon-tax-sparked-gilets-jaunes-protests-but-popular-climate-policy-is-possible-108437

President Emmanuel Macron was giving tax breaks[27] that benefitted the wealthiest French people. Macron is a lot like Trudeau: He's charmed the media by being young and cool, and he is fixated on climate causes, too. Like Trudeau, he was also born into a wealthy family and is completely out of touch with the struggles of everyday people. In France, they call him "president for the rich."[28]

French government regulations required all drivers to have high-visibility yellow vests in their vehicles to wear in case they had to get out of their vehicles on the road for an emergency. They were such a perfect symbol of the working-class truckers and labourers who were being steamrolled by elitist policies that fell heaviest on the working class while barely affecting the politicians and wealthy people who supported them. It was a way to feel like they were virtuous for caring about the climate, while not giving a damn about their fellow citizens. Exactly like here in Canada.

The movement became huge in France. It drew massive support from people on the left as well as the right. Their cause grew from protesting carbon tax to taking on the rising cost of living across France, including wages, bank fees, and the inequality between France's elitist class, pandered to by Macron, and the working people. The turnouts were massive — hundreds of thousands of people showed up, blocking roads and fuel depots for weeks on end, every Saturday, week after week, from November 2018 to March 2020. It's a good thing for Trudeau that he doesn't have to deal with angry French protesters because they were a lot less peaceful than the Freedom Convoy: there were riots, fires and looting. It only took some peaceful truckers hanging around Ottawa for Trudeau to freak out and invoke the Emergencies Act for the first time in Canadian history. Imagine if he had to face the kind of rioting they had in France: he'd be calling in airstrikes. But even Macron didn't resort to freezing the bank accounts of Yellow Vest-

27 https://www.reuters.com/article/france-tax-idINKBN1XT2D6

28 https://www.reuters.com/article/uk-france-macron-banks-idUKKBN1OA26D

supporting grandmas and grandpas. Instead, he pushed France's banks to promise to lower their fees[29], which was one of the issues people were protesting. Imagine that! He actually listened to their concerns, and tried to work with them.

Given that Canadians were also suffering badly from rising carbon taxes and growing inequality between the establishment elites and the working people, it's no surprise that the Yellow Vests inspired people here. They were having rallies every Saturday and because I knew some of the people helping make it happen, I got involved too. I started going to rallies, And I met some great people there, Cindy Parker and Ken Goldade, who would be a big part of the Freedom Convoy a few years later. The rallies were entirely about protesting Trudeau's policies. We were fighting against the carbon tax and bills C-69 and C-48. We also protested against Trudeau's assault on freedom of speech through media bailouts, which have only further corrupted our formerly free press, and speech policing, like M-103, a Parliamentary motion that promoted blasphemy laws targeting anyone who the government decided was too Islamophobic. So naturally the Liberals and some people in the media immediately began vilifying us and calling us racists and white supremacists. It was the exact same playbook they would use three years later against the Freedom Convoy.

I started helping out the Yellow Vests with the social media part, promoting the Yellow Vest movement, and organizing rallies, and helping to find people to speak at them. And I even helped organize a little pro-oil-and-gas convoy, rolling our trucks through Medicine Hat to raise awareness for our cause, which was a lot of fun, and something else that foreshadowed what would happen a few years later.

And it was at a rally in Medicine Hat where I finally got up and made my first political speech (I had to borrow someone's yellow vest first). Looking back on it now, there's a lot of meaning in the words I

29 https://www.reuters.com/article/uk-france-macron-banks-idUKKBN1OA26D

said. I wrote it as an apology to my friends and fellow Canadians for not getting politically involved sooner, because, truth be told, with all the terrible things that Trudeau had been doing, I really had never done a thing about it. It took the Yellow Vests to inspire me, just like the Yellow Vests in France had inspired my friends.

I apologized for not stepping up when Trudeau humiliated our veterans and abandoned our seniors. Here's what I said:

"I stood by and watched the Liberal government with their … division tactics trying to split us all apart and I did nothing because I thought somebody else would take care of the problem. And nobody was stepping up. I thought somebody in government would step up and nobody did…

"I stood by and I watched as my countrymen and women began to lose their jobs at an alarming rate. I had people bringing their resumes into my office two weeks before Christmas because they lost their jobs from paid [anti-oil] activism.

"I owe you all an apology for standing by and doing nothing, because I believed that somebody else would take care of the problem

"I am somebody else. And you guys are somebody else. And we can look after this as long as we keep showing up and keep supporting each other. Because we can make this change happen."

And I believed it. I believed we were making a difference. That the government would have to listen to us.

I was wrong.

CHAPTER 2:

BREEDING CHIHUAHUAS

It's easy to convince yourself you're winning, even when you're losing.

I thought we were making a difference with those Yellow Vest rallies and I had fun doing them and made some great friends. It seemed like the movement had momentum. There were other convoys happening around the province and soon there was talk of a United We Roll convoy in February 2019, and nearly 200 trucks and semis driving out to Ottawa to hold two-days of rallies on Parliament Hill.

At the time, I thought it was great. I was happy to see people getting together and doing something for the good of their fellow Canadians.

But eventually I realized the truth: it didn't make any difference. They drove all the way out there, they stayed there for a few days, and ... politically or legislatively nothing really came of it although Canadians showed up in large numbers to support them along the way.

Glen Carritt, the former Innisfail, Alta. city councillor who headed up the organizing for *United We Roll,* told reporters[30] afterward that he thought it was "100 per cent, unequivocally" a success. "Because of all the Canadian people we met along the way, right from the day we left

30 https://www.cbc.ca/news/canada/calgary/alberta-united-we-roll-convoy-organizer-1.5031454

… and all the people we saw in Ontario. That's what it was all about, all of those people we saw."

But it didn't change a thing about what Trudeau was doing to us.

Our Saturday rallies in Medicine Hat started just drawing the same people week after week.

They didn't solve anything. Trudeau's tanker ban is now enshrined in law. His pipeline gender tests are still in effect, even though an Alberta court found it unconstitutional. The Supreme Court will probably find a way to rule in favour of the law anyway. Don't forget that an Alberta court ruled that his carbon tax was unconstitutional too, but Trudeau appealed it to the Supreme Court and the judges there simply found a way to overrule it.

And in the summer of 2022, they announced more limits on the oil and gas industry with a new emissions cap specifically targeted at Alberta[31] and no other Canadian sector.

Eventually the Yellow Vest movement kind of fizzled out. The United We Roll convoy dispersed in February 2019. And a few weeks after that, things would get much, much worse. Worse than any of us could ever imagine.

When the COVID pandemic started in China, I had been working for STEP Energy Services in Medicine Hat for a couple of years since they opened up a branch office in the city. Our base was just a small satellite office, with just about 60 of us there, mostly working on the crews.

I had worked as a dispatcher for the frac crews at Schlumberger, and at STEP my official role was service administrator. It wasn't quite as fast-paced as frac logistics but I loved it all the same and worked with great people. I was the only female working out of our base at the time and was always treated with respect; I saw none of that "toxic masculinity" I kept reading about. Also during this time, I was working

31 https://calgaryherald.com/opinion/columnists/braid-the-high-cost-of-regional-bias-in-climate-change-action

as a fitness trainer and an educator on the side, and my husband and I were playing in a rock band. Life was busy, but it was rewarding.

Like you probably were, in early 2020 I was watching with concern reports out of China about a new, quickly spreading virus that was said to be very dangerous. A friend of mine kept sharing these videos making the rounds online of people in China falling over and dying in the street.

But right away, something felt off. The media started circulating what I called "fear porn" 24 hours a day. The bombardment of COVID-19 information on TV, the radio and social media was never ending. There were posters and billboards up wherever you looked. It was almost as if they wanted everyone to freak out and it seemed to be working. I was a little alarmed because we didn't know anything at that point, but it all felt a little strange and I had a nagging feeling that some things didn't make sense.

For instance, our local radio station Rock 105.3 was up until then, like the name says, a rock music station. But all of a sudden it had transformed itself into a 24/7 COVID information station. They started reporting on COVID deaths, you know, in between singles from Bryan Adams and Def Leppard.

So I started thinking, OK, but if you're going to report on every single COVID death, then I want to know how many people were killed in drunk driving accidents that day, how many people died of cancer that day, how many people died of the flu, (oh right, we eradicated the flu, never mind) and heart attacks, and strokes.

Let's put this into perspective. Do you know what the top two causes of death were in Canada in the four years before the COVID-19 pandemic began, according to Statistics Canada?[32] Cancer and heart disease. Do you know what the top two causes of death were in Canada were in 2020? Cancer and heart disease. About as many people were listed as dying from COVID in 2020 (16,151) as died

32 https://www150.statcan.gc.ca/t1/tbl1/en/tv.action?pid=1310039401

from "unintentional injuries" (15,508) — in accidents. And, of course, we know that all those who died from COVID didn't just die from COVID. Among people who were recorded as dying "from COVID" who were older than 85 years old, Statistics Canada reported[33], 89 per cent had comorbidities: diabetes, Alzheimer's disease, hypertension, heart disease, or any number of other very serious ailments. Under the age of 45, people with other serious conditions accounted for 100 per cent of "COVID deaths."

It became obvious from the start of the pandemic that this was a disease that was a risk for elderly people who had other complicating issues. I wouldn't wish death on anyone, and I feel terrible for the people who died and their families. But even as the World Health Organization was declaring COVID-19 a global pandemic, the advice was already abundantly clear that it was high-risk people who needed protection[34].

And the world seemed to be going absolutely crazy. They were holding hundreds of Canadians as effective prisoners on cruise ships, and then flying them into military bases where they were held prisoner again for two weeks[35] (even though the vast majority of people on cruise ships that had COVID outbreaks never even ended up getting COVID). In February, then-federal health minister Patty Hajdu, who has absolutely no background in health, was telling people to stockpile food and medication. A professor at the University of British Columbia even coined the phrase "coronaphobia,"[36] which he concluded was having a "a significant psychological impact" on Canadian society. It seemed like a science fiction movie, where some alien virus makes the population deranged. And to me, it was starting to feel just as

33 https://twitter.com/fordnation/status/1244686770681323528?lang=en

34 https://twitter.com/fordnation/status/1244686770681323528?lang=en

35 https://toronto.citynews.ca/2020/03/10/coronavirus-grand-princess-cruise-ship-cfb-trenton/

36 https://www.ncbi.nlm.nih.gov/pmc/articles/PMC7134790/

contrived. I just thought, "This is madness." I'm not a scientist or a doctor, obviously, but it didn't make sense to me.

Then, in March 2020, Justin Trudeau and his finance minister at the time, Bill Morneau, met with a small group of MPs and tried to use the pandemic to sneak through Bill C-13. It was a undemocratic bill that would have given the finance minister the right to spend money and raise taxes however he wanted, without parliamentary oversight, until the end of 2021.[37] It seemed to me that anyone who didn't think there were a whole lot of things going on that we should be suspicious about clearly wasn't paying attention.

And then the economic impact hit. The price of oil started going down because China's economy was locked down at the end of January. Here in Alberta, producers started pulling back. STEP sent their employees home to work remotely. I worked from home for about two weeks when they announced they were shutting operations at our Medicine Hat base and closed the shop, with the bulk of our local staff being laid off. My husband, Dwayne, an oilfield mechanic, was laid off, too.

Then they started the lockdowns. In Alberta that meant closing restaurants and bars, banquet halls, conference centres, trade shows, concert venues, markets and community centres. Sports were banned. Stores were forced to impose safety restrictions and allow only a small number of customers at a time. Churches were closed.

Medicine Hat became like a ghost town. Dwayne and I lost every single avenue of income that we had. We both worked in the oil and gas industry, which was devastated. I also worked in fitness, and the gyms were closed. And all the venues that hired live music were closed down.

We had nothing to do except to apply for the federal handouts that Trudeau was making us all dependent on, so we headed off to

37 https://calgaryherald.com/news/local-news/corbella-trudeaus-attempted-power-grab-an-alarming-breach-of-trust

Manitoba to visit my daughter and her fiancé on their farm. When we arrived, we found out they were expecting a baby the following November and we decided to return to Medicine Hat, pack up a few more things and head back and help on the farm where we could. The cities and towns were like ghost towns and there was much more freedom on the farm.

We helped feed the livestock, and Dwayne taught me how to drive a tractor. We walked the fence line, a lot of it in the bush, and made repairs. Dwayne helped with seeding and haying, fixed up the equipment when it broke and generally just tried to be productive. We spent time down at the lake, out on the boat fishing, and taking the side-by-side out so I could pick wild flowers.

Manitoba was very militant with their mask mandates and, living in a really small community like that, if you didn't put a mask on, you didn't get groceries. We kept our social circle quite small, but we still had friendly get-togethers and the occasional jam.

The whole mask thing was another thing that didn't make sense to me. In Manitoba, even some of the rural people were masking up and lecturing you about masks, because that's what they believed would protect them, like it was some kind of magic fabric. But when the whole pandemic started, the public health officials were telling us masks were useless.

"Absolutely we want to protect our frontline health-care workers and prioritizing supply in that setting is critically important," is what federal Chief Public Health Officer Theresa Tam said in March 2020[38]. "Putting a mask on an asymptomatic person is not beneficial obviously if you're not infected." Alberta's health officials said the same thing: "Masks are intended to protect others from your illness. Albertans are generally not advised to wear a mask if you are healthy."[39]

---

38 https://www.cbc.ca/player/play/1717905987907

39 https://calgary.ctvnews.ca/alberta-health-says-face-masks-only-required-if-you-are-sick-1.4881751

Then suddenly they all changed their minds. Not only that, they started making it sound like this virus was so dangerous, you should wear them while you were having sex.[40] Tam went from saying in March that you didn't need to bother unless you were sick, to saying in September that you should even wear them during sex — but you could still have sex! Public health officials even started talking about "choosing sexual positions that limit face-to-face contact" and "Use barriers like walls (e.g., glory holes), that allow for sexual contact but prevent close face-to-face contact."[41]

All of a sudden this virus is so dangerous that we need to stand behind walls and use "glory holes" to have sex with each other, but a piece of fabric on our mouth will also magically protect us. We've all seen those hazmat suits that they have to wear in a virology lab. If this virus was really as transmissible and dangerous as they were making it sound, then why would a flimsy mask protect us? Either they were misleading us about how dangerous it was, or they were misleading us about the masks, or they were misleading us about both. But it became clear to me that they were misleading us about something.

Even though I had no confidence in the masking rules, you might be surprised to learn that I followed them when I had to. I wasn't one of the people getting into fights with the clerks at the grocery store. I was never a jerk about it. If a store or a health clinic or something said they required me to wear a mask, then I put on a mask. I'd take it off the second I walked out the door. But I wasn't about to ruin the day of some grocery clerk or nurse. These people were having a hard enough time working through all this as it was.

The thing about the mask mandates, that I'm sure more and more people are realizing, is that they were a step in the process of getting us all used to being controlled, a process that would eventually end

---

40 https://www.canada.ca/en/public-health/news/2020/09/statement-from-the-chief-public-health-officer-of-canada-on-september-2-2020.html

41 https://www.vancouverisawesome.com/bc-news/bc-health-officials-tips-safe-sex-during-covid-19-pandemic-2580596

up with people being denied their livelihoods if they didn't get a government-enforced injection. As someone once said, the best way to control people is to take away a little of their freedom at a time.

Don't get me wrong, you might choose to wear a mask, and I have absolutely no problem with that. You might be in one of those higher-risk categories, or you're around people who are, or you just find that it makes you feel safer. I'm not going to make someone feel badly for wearing a mask. I still see people even now wearing masks, even when they're walking outside and that's their choice, and I respect it. My oldest daughter is a nurse and she works for Alberta Health Services and she is very much in favour of masking and vaccination, and I respect her, and she respects me (we're also both very respectful of avoiding getting into debates with each other). That's freedom. And if there's one thing I believe in, it's that everyone should have the freedom to make their own choices.

During the Freedom Convoy, I heard stories, although I never saw it myself and I have no idea if they're true, about protesters giving a hard time to some of the staff at local stores or their customers for wearing masks. I have no patience for that. I also don't know if those people were truckers. We had a lot of enemies circulating around the protest who were there to agitate, posing as if they might be truckers, just to give us a bad name, and the media fell for it. There were people arrested who the media said were with the Freedom Convoy, but it would later turn out they weren't. It was definitely one of the tactics that Antifa was using.

It doesn't matter whether you're pro-government or anti-government, no one can deny that the masks, along with the 24/7 fear porn on the radio and television, the daily reports of case counts and death counts, the wildly overinflated projections of casualties that never even came close to coming true, and the grim-looking politicians warning us daily of mass death and destruction if we didn't do what they told us, this all had the effect of making our society into one of terrified and timid animals. The worst of them began turning on anyone who they felt weren't following the rules.

When I was living on the farm in Manitoba during the first part of the lockdowns, I eventually applied for, and was offered a position with the local municipality. I was eager to get off of the federal CERB — the Canadian Emergency Response Benefit — as soon as possible.

I recall while working there around Christmastime I took a few "snitch" calls from people reporting on other people for not following public health rules. There was one in particular that stuck with me. A woman called the office to report there were four cars parked in the driveway of an Airbnb near her house, which looked to her like a violation of the restrictions on gatherings. Of course, I was professional. I did my job, took the phone call and passed on the information. But, in my mind, I was thinking, it's Christmastime, for crying out loud. This family probably hasn't seen each other in a year and they're just trying to have a family Christmas. You don't have to go over there. You don't have to interact with them. What the hell is your problem?

Our once freedom-loving Canadian society was turning into something I didn't recognize. In what seemed like just a few months we had degenerated into a population that locked itself away in fear, where people hid their faces whenever they dared to venture out, and viciously turned on anyone who dared to show any sign of disobedience or independence.

Little did I know that it was about to get much, much worse.

As I've learned more about my Métis heritage, I've been compelled by my Native origins. It was a calling in my literal blood. And for Native people, a sacred animal is the wolf.

The piercing eyes of a wolf surveys the land, over which they cover great distances. On their hunts they naturally form into perfect hierarchies, within which each animal knows its role. They are naturally beautiful creatures who need the expanse, and the limitless horizon, to survive.

But consider a little dog, like a chihuahua, in some 600-square foot condo in downtown Toronto or Vancouver. The chihuahua trembles all the time, and it cries. It has separation anxiety. When he wants to eat, he has to beg. When he wants to pee, he must ask for permission, and if he doesn't and pees where he shouldn't, he is scolded and shamed. When the owner is mad, the dog must keep its distance, and crawl into his cage.

In other words, the chihuahua is completely domesticated. He could never live freely on his own, even if he wanted to. Without a master, he will die. And yet that pitiful chihuahua is a descendant of the noble wolf. With just enough generations of domestication, even the most powerful, independent animal can completely degenerate. It can be made into helpless creature that looks at the world not with courage, but with terror.

So, was this fear and terror that had seemingly gripped society even that hard to predict? Or was it just the latest step in a process that had begun even before?

Even before COVID turned up on the scene, things were already diseased. The obesity pandemic was around long before the coronavirus. Our kids are experiencing chronic ailments historically reserved for the elderly. Generalized anxiety and depression are at a catastrophic high. If some kids can't sit still for 12 hours a day, if they're too active, too independent, then we put them on Adderall.

And for the stuff we don't have drugs for, we just lower our standards. We drop the bar. We eliminate entry requirements for educational programs. We give out trophies and awards for showing up.

As I mentioned earlier, before the pandemic hit I was working on the side a little bit as a personal fitness trainer, in addition to my day job in the oil sector. It wasn't much, because I didn't have a lot of time. Often I'd be up at 4:30 am and not be done my day until nine or 10 o'clock at night. And you can't really make that much money doing fitness training in a little place like Medicine Hat, with a population of 65,000.

I wasn't in it for the money. I was in it because I loved watching my clients transform before my eyes. Another part of it was that I just loved working with people, and how we'd come to trust each other, and they would let me into their lives and tell me things in confidence about themselves and their personal lives and their problems. But what was most rewarding was seeing people building themselves up. When we put in the work, they would become stronger, not just physically, but mentally. They would feel better. Their confidence would grow. And because of that, they became happier. And being stronger, more confident and happier made them better equipped to deal with the challenges and problems in their lives.

And one of the first things the government took away from us during the pandemic was fitness and sports, when they closed the gyms, banned indoor personal training and shut down sports leagues. The very places where people could become stronger, physically and mentally. And of course, they banned worship services, the very places where people could become stronger spiritually. And they closed businesses, the place where we are at our strongest providing for ourselves and our families.

Staying home and sitting on the couch watching TV and eating potato chips used to be something that we frowned on. Suddenly it was recast as selfless and noble. One German ad campaign called "Together against Corona #SpecialHeroes" even ran ads celebrating couch potatoes[42], featuring old people in the future telling war stories of their bravery during the pandemic for doing absolutely nothing. "Suddenly the fate of this country lay in our hands," says one. "So we mustered all our courage and did what was expected of us, the only right thing. We did nothing. Absolutely nothing. We were like lazy raccoons," and the ad flashed back to a young man in his prime

42 https://www.youtube.com/watch?v=FS1DDn2eklU

lying on a couch drinking soda, surrounded by dirty dishes, watching television. "Days and nights we stayed on our backsides at home and fought against the spread of the coronavirus… this is how we became heroes." The tagline? "Be lazy, save lives."

Here in Canada, Trudeau officially endorsed the message, and retweeted the ad. "Have you seen Germany's new ads about COVID-19? It doesn't matter what language you speak, the message is clear. You can be the hero in the fight against this virus — and you don't even have to do that much," Trudeau tweeted.[43]

Of course, this wasn't actually true for a whole lot of people. Farmers didn't stay home and watch TV on their couches. They kept working, so people could have food to eat on their couches. Truck drivers didn't "sit on their backsides at home" either. They drove the rigs that kept the groceries coming. And there were millions more people who showed up for work everyday, too, who absolutely deserve our praise: grocery store clerks, bus drivers, medical and support staff, and many, many more.

But those ads, and Trudeau's messaging, and the whole effort to celebrate laziness, those weren't actually meant for people who work with their hands and work on their feet all day, because those people weren't staying home. They couldn't stay home. The ads were meant for a certain class of people: the laptop class. These are the people who had the privilege of staying home, collecting government handouts or working remotely from their portable computers, ordering stuff from Amazon and Wayfair, without leaving the comfort of their homes. The pro-lazy messaging was designed explicitly to make them feel like they were the real stars of the show.

These are the people who would post on Facebook about how the lockdowns had been a wonderful way to spend more time with their families. They proudly posted on Instagram photos from their new baking hobby taken up in lockdown, and how rewarding they found

43 https://twitter.com/JustinTrudeau/status/1328510550209417217?ref_

it. And these are the people are politicians cared about, because these are the people who controlled the dialogue, who championed more lockdowns, even though the shutdowns overwhelmingly affected blue-collar workers and small-business owners. But people working remotely also reported "more anxiety, burnout, fatigue, lack of purpose, and overall imbalance in their lives."[44]

Then people started putting on weight. A 2021 *Dalhousie University* study[45] found that, in just the first year of the pandemic, more than 40 per cent of Canadians reported "unintentional weight gain," with 39 per cent of Canadians saying they had gained at least 11 pounds. And, not surprising in the least, people started drinking more, with nearly a quarter of people reporting greater alcohol consumption in the first year, according to another study. Scientific evidence suggests that after about two months, such habits can become engrained. Some Canadians were under stay-at-home orders that amounted to much longer than that.[46]

The worst of it, of course, was the horrific opioid pandemic that swept our country, and others, taking thousands of lives while barely meriting a mention in the media that was too occupied reporting COVID case counts 24/7. It turns out that if you lock people up so they become more anxious and imbalanced and lacking purpose in life, and then send them thousands of dollars in government cheques, some of them end up with dangerous drug addictions.

During the first year of the pandemic alone, there was a 96-per-cent increase in opioid overdoses in the first year of the pandemic, *Statistics Canada* reported.[47] Most of them were among exactly the kind of people most likely to find themselves feeling most unhappy,

---

44 https://cdn.dal.ca/content/dam/dalhousie/pdf/sites/agri-food/COVID%20Well%20Being%20(April%2018%202021)%20EN.pdf

45 https://www.bbc.com/news/world-us-canada-57079577

46 https://www.bbc.com/news/world-us-canada-57079577

47 https://health-infobase.canada.ca/substance-related-harms/opioids-stimulants/

isolated, spiritless and purposeless during lockdowns: working-age men. According to the Statistics Canada data, 74 per cent of opioid overdose deaths between April 2020 and March 2021 were among men, the majority of them aged 20 to 59 years old.

The destructive cycle of degradation and domestication was feeding on itself. The more anxious the laptop class became from being at home all the time, the more freaked-out they were about COVID. The more freaked-out they were, the more they demanded more government restrictions to protect them. The more unhealthy, out-of-shape and fatigued they became, the more their lives became small and the less confidence they had. The less confidence they had, the more scared and desperate they grew. The more they lacked purpose in their lives, the more their purpose became all about following the government's pandemic rules. The more heroic they were made to feel about their laziness, the more they lectured and attacked and demeaned those people who refused to submit to government control.

And surprise, surprise. By the time the vaccines started rolling out, instead of getting better, everything got worse. A lot worse. The toxic us-versus-them dynamic that had been nourished and cultivated by government rules and messaging only intensified, even as the flip-flops and mixed messaging from officials got even weirder.

The first vaccine in Canada was AstraZeneca and we were told it was safe. Then we were told it wasn't. Then it was safe, again. Then it wasn't, again. The vaccines were going to stop the pandemic, then they weren't, then we needed two, then we needed three. The mRNA vaccines were 100-per-cent safe, until there were reports of myocarditis, thrombosis and deaths.[48] The vaccines would put an end to the pandemic. Then they only worked for a while, for some people, for some strains.

---

48 https://www.cdc.gov/coronavirus/2019-ncov/vaccines/safety/adverse-events.html

And then there was the most audacious lie of all: That the government wasn't going to force you to get a vaccine. Trudeau had said as much in an interview on the *Brandon Gonez Show* in May 2021[49], when he said he was "really worried" about people being banned from going to a Raptors game for not being vaccinated: "We're not a country that makes vaccination mandatory," he said.

Then before we knew it, the government was going to force us to get one, not just to go to a basketball or a hockey game or a restaurant or a movie or get on a plane or a train. Hundreds of thousands of Canadians were being told that if they didn't get vaccinated, they'd lose their jobs, and the federal government would deny them access to their employment insurance.[50] They were being ordered to obey the government's order to inject themselves with a novel serum, without any data of long-term effects, that many of us didn't want or didn't trust, or lose their livelihoods.

A lot of people, degraded and debilitated by what had by then been nearly 18 months of demeaning government control, went along with it. They made their appointments. They got their shots. They did as they were told. The government tweeted its approval.[51]

But then it all went horribly wrong for Trudeau's government after he made what will go down as the biggest mistake of his political career.

He tried messing with the wrong people.

He tried messing with truckers.

49 https://www.youtube.com/watch?v=qjpFe1fdhxU

50 https://www.benefitscanada.com/human-resources/hr-law/unvaccinated-employees-may-not-be-eligible-for-ei-feds/

51 https://twitter.com/JustinTrudeau/status/1478384335841644547

CHAPTER 3:

'WHEN IS ENOUGH ENOUGH?'

Stop for a moment and think about how many people our governments were able to punish for their personal choices before people finally stood up to them.

First they came for the health-care workers who, for any number of valid and important personal reasons, did not want to be injected with the government-ordered mRNA vaccine. Not just doctors and nurses, but also medical laboratory staff, medical students, long-term care workers, assisted-care workers, hospital social workers and still others.[52]They were all told they had to get the COVID shot or lose their jobs.

Only in Quebec, where the government feared a shortage of workers, did hospitals eventually back off from enforcing mandates — after nearly three months of threatening people's careers. (Although the province required that to be hired as a new health-care worker you had to get the vaccines.[53]) Meanwhile, in Ontario, Premier Doug Ford didn't want to defend the mandates so he downloaded it onto hospitals, telling them to fire unvaccinated workers themselves. In all

52 https://www.albertahealthservices.ca/news/Page16165.aspx

53 https://www.cbc.ca/news/canada/montreal/mandatory-vaccination-new-health-workers-1.6235760

of Ontario, only one hospital, in the small town of Hearst, opposed the mandates.[54]

Then they came for the government employees. This included the RCMP and the military. The same people who our country relies on to dangerously put themselves in the line of fire if we need them to, were told they weren't allowed to choose to take their chances with an overwhelmingly survivable respiratory virus that posed no meaningful risk to young, healthy people. They were ordered instead to take a novel and uncertain injection or get thrown out of the service.

They came for the airline workers.

And the police forces.

And the firefighters and paramedics.

And bus drivers and garbage collectors.

And teachers.

And university students.

These were millions of people in the public sector alone. There were millions more in the private sector facing the same ultimatum: inject yourself with the government-ordered shot or lose your livelihood.

Now stop for a moment and imagine how much further it could have gone.

One by one, every single guardrail that Canadians had counted on to hold government power in check had failed completely. The celebrated Charter of Rights and Freedoms, that we had all learned in school was Canada's most glorious legacy, supposedly a model that free countries everywhere admired and sought to emulate, proved utterly worthless. The Charter had one job: protecting individual rights against government abuses and the tyranny of the majority. It failed miserably.

Citizens were stopped by police if they were suspected of nothing more than gathering with their fellow citizens, a right supposedly

54 https://toronto.citynews.ca/2022/02/01/ontario-hospitals-vaccine-mandate-doug-ford/

guaranteed by the Charter's protection of our right to assembly and association. Men gathering to play basketball were charged.[55] People from different families were ticketed if they were seen in cars together. People were prosecuted for attending what the law now called "illegal gatherings." Before governments began locking us down, there were no such thing as illegal gatherings. Any gathering was guaranteed as legal, we were told by the Charter.

The right to mobility is also supposedly guaranteed by our Charter. Except police stopped and punished people for going to public parks.[56] And exercising.[57] For walking their dog. And playing outside with their kids.[58] Our Charter-enshrined rights to leave the country and to return to it were all just tossed away in an instant. As in the old East Germany, without government approval, free citizens were stopped from leaving the country, while others were stopped from re-entering.

Our right to practice our religions was shredded. Parishioners and preachers were persecuted for holding worship services.

Calgary pastor Tim Stephens was arrested in front of his crying children and held in custody for weeks for holding "illegal" services.[59] He was even arrested for holding them outdoors.

---

55 https://tnc.news/2020/04/07/5-cases-of-people-fined-for-not-social-distancing/

56 https://www.cbc.ca/news/canada/ottawa/here-s-where-ottawans-are-being-fined-for-hanging-out-in-parks-1.5541552

57 https://www.narcity.com/toronto/a-toronto-social-distancing-fine-was-given-to-a-man-for-exercising-alone-in-a-park

58 https://tnc.news/2020/04/07/5-cases-of-people-fined-for-not-social-distancing/

59 https://globalnews.ca/news/7950499/calgary-pastor-tim-stephens-arrested-covid-19-june-14/

Edmonton-area pastor James Coates was arrested and jailed[60] for holding so-called illegal services and his church was confiscated by the province for months.

In Canada, there didn't used to be any such thing as illegal religious services.

Calgary pastor Artur Pawlowski, who fled Communist Poland as a youth, was fined tens of thousands of dollars, arrested five times and jailed for daring to organize Christian worship.[61] A judge even ordered him, on pain of law, to start preaching things he didn't believe in[62], insisting Pawlowski promote social distancing and vaccination. So much for the Charter's protection of "freedom of thought, belief, opinion and expression."

James Topp also knows how hollow that supposed right has proven to be. The Canadian soldier is facing a court martial[63] for speaking out against vaccine mandates. Another soldier, military reservist officer cadet Laszlo Kenderesi, who also grew up under Soviet oppression, was literally charged by the military with mutiny[64] for expressing his opinion opposing the COVID injections. He was actually charged with mutiny for expressing a personal opinion.

Along with the total failure of the once-revered Charter, the courts, another supposed check against government oppression, also did nothing. Actually, the courts did worse than nothing: they publicly endorsed the violations of our rights. They ordered Artur Pawlowski to parrot government talking points. They ruled against citizens fined for refusing to submit to COVID tests. And they ruled against

---

60 https://nationalpost.com/opinion/kristopher-kinsinger-the-arrest-of-alberta-pastor-james-coates-is-a-constitutional-abnormality

61 https://www.foxnews.com/world/pastor-running-office-welcomes-plan-pardon-covid-offenders-being-jailed-keeping-church-open

62 https://www.thelawyersdaily.ca/articles/30594/probation-order-in-alberta-covid-19-protest-case-raising-free-speech-concerns

63 https://globalnews.ca/news/8970677/james-topp-court-martial/

64 https://www.durhamradionews.com/archives/159683

citizens denied access to work or university education for refusing to be vaccinated.

The courts upheld punishments against churches and businesspeople exercising their rights to assembly, commerce and association. Our courts endorsed the restrictions on travel and the fines for those who refused to submit to the orders of border guards. When a terminally ill patient in Alberta was denied access to a lifesaving organ transplant because she wouldn't agree to take a COVID shot first[65], the courts said that was just fine, too.

And the news media, instead of upholding their responsibility of holding our government to account for authoritarian overreach, did the opposite: They held to account those citizens who refused to comply with official public health decrees, while dismissing and mocking any skepticism about masks, lockdowns and mandates.

In August 2021, the *Toronto Star* ran on its front page[66] in giant display type, around a story about the "simmering divide" over vaccines, headlines saying: "I have no empathy left for the wilfully unvaccinated. Let them die… Unvaccinated patients do not deserve ICU beds." One of Quebec's most popular talk show hosts[67] used her show as a platform to promote forced vaccinations and the arrest of unvaccinated people.

And I'm still in utter disbelief about how every major labour union refused to fight for their workers' right to make their own personal medical choices. Instead, these so-called workers unions fully supported any employers who demanded that staff get injected or get fired. I thought that standing up for their members was the whole reason unions existed. Unifor, Canada's largest private sector union, literally

---

65 https://edmontonjournal.com/news/crime/court-upholds-doctors-right-to-require-covid-vaccination-for-organ-transplant-patient-saying-alternative-is-medical-chaos

66 https://thestarepaper.pressreader.com/toronto-star/20210826

67 https://tnc.news/2022/01/20/viewers-push-back-against-quebec-tv-show-where-kids-called-for-forced-vaccination/

states on its website[68] that part of its official mission is "working with our members to improve their rights in the workplace." But in October 2021, Unifor issued a statement[69] saying it was taking "a position in favour of workplace mandatory vaccine policies."

After the failure of the Charter, the courts, the media and labour unions, there was virtually nothing left standing in the way of governments going even further than they had. Even the Catholic Church, whose power of resistance had helped to defeat European communism, said that mass vaccination was a "moral obligation."[70]

Thousands of people lost their jobs because of their refusal to get the government-enforced injection. And pollsters were busily amassing ammunition that would only help politicians expand the mandates.

The Trudeau government had announced[71] that by early 2022 it would start requiring anyone working for an industry that was federally regulated to get the injection or lose their jobs. In Canada, that encompasses 1.3 million workers in a huge swath of businesses: banks, air transport, port services, postal and courier services, railways, radio and television broadcasting, telecommunications, certain types of mining, certain types of agriculture, certain oil and gas activities, and more. It would also include all 47 Crown corporations.

And there's no reason to think the government would stop there. Trudeau had campaigned in the 2021 election on a platform of vilifying the unvaccinated and punishing them as much as possible. He promised[72] a federal fund that would award money to provinces

---

68 https://www.unifor.org/about-us/history-mission

69 https://www.unifor.org/news/all-news/open-letter-unifor-local-unions-activists-and-staff

70 https://www.cbcew.org.uk/wp-content/uploads/sites/3/2020/03/catholic-position-on-vaccination-110820.pdf

71 https://mcmillan.ca/insights/mandatory-vaccination-for-federally-regulated-workplaces-coming-early-2022/

72 https://ici.radio-canada.ca/rci/en/news/1822121/trudeau-ratchets-up-talk-on-mandatory-vaccinations-says-hell-protect-businesses-people-from-lawsuits

for implementing strict vaccine passports and vowed to pass laws exempting businesses from any legal challenges they might face over strict mandates. The Quebec government had already announced that it would be implementing a special tax just on unvaccinated people, which Trudeau had good things to say about[73], and pollsters[74] soon found[75] a majority of Canadians supported the idea.

Trudeau had campaigned on banning unvaccinated people from travel, which he immediately did after winning the election, barring anyone who would not prove their vaccination status from travelling by planes and trains. People who refused to be injected with novel vaccines were being robbed of their freedom to even travel to visit their families.

Still more chillingly, he used the election to try to dehumanize anyone who didn't want the injection. "They don't believe in science [and] progress and are very often misogynistic and racist," he told a Quebec television show.[76] "This leads us, as a leader and as a country, to make a choice: Do we tolerate these people?" Whether Trudeau realizes it or not, history tells us that the denigration of a certain segment of society and raising the question of whether they should even be allowed to exist have often been a prelude to grave atrocities. It was an alarming new low.

Unfortunately, history also tells us that ugly, naked discrimination can often be popular, especially in times of perceived crisis. And the Trudeau government, along with governments across Canada, had succeeded in terrifying people into accepting that COVID was an

73 https://www.ctvnews.ca/health/coronavirus/quebec-s-tax-on-unvaccinated-trudeau-says-strong-measures-have-worked-1.5737100

74 https://www.ipsos.com/en-ca/news-and-polls/half-of-canadians-agree-government-should-enact-a-tax-on-unvaccinated-people

75 https://toronto.citynews.ca/2022/01/12/canada-poll-unvaccinated-fines/

76 https://www.westernstandard.news/news/trudeau-calls-the-unvaccinated-racist-and-misogynistic-extremists/article_a3bacece-2e14-5b8c-bf37-eddd672205f3.html

unprecedented and ruinous crisis. So it was, sadly, all too predictable when the Angus Reid Institute polled Canadians in late 2021[77] and found a strong majority wholeheartedly in support of "workers being fired" from their jobs for refusing vaccinations. Not just medical professionals, but everyone from restaurant employees to "people who work for small private businesses in your community." They should all be forced to get an injection, most Canadians said, or lose their jobs.

So, as the country entered 2022, after nearly two years of pandemic and restrictions, the push towards more mandates, more passports, more punishments for the unvaccinated seemed to be only gaining momentum at a frightening rate.

Certain communities had already started banning the unvaccinated from public services[78], including libraries and museums. And in addition to its tax on the unvaccinated, Quebec had also begun barring unvaccinated people from liquor and cannabis stores.[79] In B.C., the government was facing pressure to follow suit.[80] Quebec also implemented a vaccine requirement for people to shop at certain stores[81], such as Walmart, Canadian Tire, Costco and even Ikea. And in New Brunswick, the health minister revealed a plan that would require proof-of-vaccination at retailers, including grocery stores.[82] They were actually trying to deny unvaccinated people access to food.

---

77 https://angusreid.org/covid-firing-booster/

78 https://kitchener.ctvnews.ca/region-of-waterloo-requiring-covid-19-vaccination-to-enter-museums-use-in-person-library-programs-1.5622691

79 https://montreal.ctvnews.ca/quebecers-will-need-to-show-vaccine-passports-to-access-liquor-cannabis-stores-1.5729843

80 https://bc.ctvnews.ca/doctor-urges-b-c-government-to-expand-vaccine-passport-to-liquor-cannabis-stores-1.5743989

81 https://montreal.ctvnews.ca/shoppers-entering-quebec-s-big-box-stores-now-must-have-covid-19-vaccine-passports-1.5751872

82 https://www.cbc.ca/news/canada/new-brunswick/pandemic-rules-civil-liberties-association-1.6284670

All around us, we were seeing glimpses of how bad things could get as the screws were being turned tighter on anyone who refused to submit to the vaccine pressure. In Austria, in November 2021, the government began experimenting with lockdowns targeted entirely at people who refused the vaccine, prohibiting them from leaving home for any reason except for a handful of government-approved "necessities."[83] People had to show their papers to authorities if they left their homes, and the fines for anyone caught violating the virtual house arrest ran up to $1,700. That same month, it was announced in Australia that anyone who hadn't received the injection would be banned from visiting not just restaurants, theatres, concerts, libraries and museums, but also hospitals, long-term care facilities, prisons and disability services.[84]

At the same time, the definition of what would count as "vaccinated" was shifting. Originally, governments only required adults to have one dose to count as vaccinated in order to be allowed to participate in the economy, but within just a few weeks[85], that was jacked up to two doses. It wasn't long before politicians were then saying that soon a third dose would be required.[86] It was obvious to anyone who cared to look that the goal posts would never stop moving. As soon as they coerced enough people into getting three doses, they would make it so you needed four doses, then five, and then six. And you had better keep up, or you'll be put under house arrest, like the unvaccinated Austrians were.

And by the start of 2022 Canada's health minister, Jean-Yves Duclos, was signalling that soon, the right to even say no to a vaccine

83 https://www.bbc.com/news/world-europe-59283128

84 https://www.abc.net.au/news/2021-11-09/qld-coronavirus-covid-restrictions-update-unvaccinated/100605840

85 https://globalnews.ca/news/8290710/alberta-covid-19-vaccine-passport-october-22-2021/

86 https://www.mtlblog.com/quebec-vaccine-passport-eventually-require-3-doses-valid

would no longer be an option at all. Vaccines, he said, would eventually have to become mandatory for everyone, whether they liked it or not. "I don't think we're there yet," he said.[87] "But I think discussions need to be had about mandatory vaccination, because we need to get rid of COVID-19."

But Duclos also eventually admitted[88] that people "will never be 'fully vaccinated' against COVID" and that Canadians would need "to keep our vaccinations up to date" by being dosed at least every nine months.

And not just adults. In Toronto, Canada's biggest city, the chief public health officer and city public health board were pressuring the province[89] to make it mandatory for kids to get the shot if they wanted to be able to go to school. The board was also pushing to eliminate exemptions[90] for any reason other than those approved by a doctor. Even religious objections would not be tolerated.

It was becoming abundantly clear that there were no lines that politicians and health officials were not prepared to cross in their fanaticism of forcing us all to get injected with their government-enforced vaccines. They would take away everything you had and make your life miserable. If that didn't work, they would use force to make you get it. And they would force your kids to do it, too. And then they would make us all do it again, and again, and again, every few months.

In the meantime, Ottawa was pushing its ArriveCAN smartphone app as a border-control measure that would determine your eligibility to travel based on whether your vaccination status met the government

---

87 https://www.ipolitics.ca/news/mandatory-vaccination-likely-coming-to-canada-health-minister

88 https://www.canada.ca/en/public-health/news/2022/07/remarks-for-the-honourable-jean-yves-duclos-minister-of-health.html

89 https://www.thestar.com/news/gta/2022/01/12/stay-tuned-toronto-public-health-still-waiting-for-details-from-province-on-back-to-school-plan.html

90 https://www.theglobeandmail.com/canada/article-debate-grows-over-mandatory-covid-19-vaccines-for-children/

requirements. The Liberals had introduced it innocently as a "voluntary alternative to contact tracing," as the scholars Bianca Wylie and Matt Malone at the respected Centre for International Governance Innovation wrote in a critical essay in September 2022.[91] "[B]ut quickly, and without any discussion, it has since transformed into a mandatory border-control app ... Its use is enforced through penalties under the Quarantine Act for 'failure to comply with an order prohibiting or subjecting to any condition the entry into Canada' that have steadily climbed from $1,000 to $3,000 to $5,000."

But as Malone has also pointed out[92], no one outside government really knows anything about the technology behind ArriveCAN. The government has designated the algorithm[93] inside it a "trade secret." There is no transparency on how the data that ArriveCAN collects are being used. And sources in Ottawa were telling reporters[94] as late as July 2022 that the data in ArriveCAN were too valuable to abandon the app, despite widespread calls[95] for its elimination, including criticism from border guards themselves. And despite the fact that it had strayed wildly from the government's original justification that it would help speed up border entry, and was making it only harder, slower and less likely for people to travel at all. In fact, the Liberals wanted to expand the app even further, to collect even more data on travellers.[96]

---

91 https://www.cigionline.org/articles/canadas-arrivecan-app-is-fostering-inequity-at-the-border/

92 https://www.ctvnews.ca/politics/canada-will-keep-arrivecan-for-its-data-%20on-covid-19-positive-travellers-sources-1.5977612

93 https://www.ctvnews.ca/politics/canada-will-keep-arrivecan-for-its-data-%20on-covid-19-positive-travellers-sources-1.5977612

94 https://www.ctvnews.ca/politics/canada-will-keep-arrivecan-for-its-data-on-covid-19-positive-travellers-sources-1.5977612

95 https://windsorstar.com/news/local-news/cbsa-union-president-calling-for-changes-to-arrivecan

96 https://nationalpost.com/news/arrivecan-app-may-stay-as-part-of-larger-border-modernization-mendicinos-comments-suggest

As 2021 rolled into 2022, approaching the second anniversary of the great Canadian pandemic panic, it truly seemed to me that there was almost nothing stopping the runaway expansion of government control into our homes, our families, our travel, our livelihoods and our medical choices. Officials seemed to be able to do whatever they wanted, grant themselves whatever abusive powers they desired, as long as they said it was needed to stop the pandemic. A state of war serves as an excuse for domestic tyranny, Aleksandr Solzhenitsyn said. And so our government learned to love the war.

What was scarier was that the more they made us miserable, the more the public became desperate to believe that every new power the government gave itself would be the way to finally end the pandemic. What was unfolding in Australia, a country just like Canada in so many ways, was a vision of a dystopian future that wasn't that far from reality here. Their liberal, democratic order had been turned into an authoritarian police state[97]: Residents were literally locked inside their homes and apartments.[98] It went on for weeks, and months. Virtually all travel in or out of the country was forbidden. The military was deployed to enforce stay-at-home orders. Anti-lockdown demonstrations were banned. People were arrested for even daring to talk online about protesting.[99] Others were investigated[100] for "liking" anti-lockdown Facebook posts.

This wasn't China: This was in an English-speaking Commonwealth "liberal democracy." Just like ours.

---

97 https://www.theatlantic.com/ideas/archive/2021/09/pandemic-australia-still-liberal-democracy/619940/

98 https://www.nytimes.com/2020/11/12/world/australia/melbourne-towers-lockdown.html

99 https://www.hrw.org/news/2020/09/24/australia-harsh-police-response-during-covid-19

100 https://fee.org/articles/australias-violent-enforcement-of-lockdowns-sparks-memories-of-the-eureka-rebellion/

Supposedly democratic governments had found a perpetual-motion machine that allowed them to justify every abuse by promising it would bring an end to the abuse. Just a little more government control, we were told, would lead us to more freedom. George Orwell would have been impressed.

Today I look back and wonder how far it would have gone if one thing hadn't changed, if Trudeau did not make his one fatal error, which brought it all crashing down.

Trudeau forgot, or thought that people wouldn't remember, that he had made heroes out of the truckers, long before he made enemies of them.

In March 2020, just a week after the World Health Organization declared COVID-19 a global pandemic, Trudeau first thanked truck drivers[101], along with first responders and health-care workers, among others who were "working overtime to keep us safe and keep the country moving."

"Thank you for being there for us," he said. "Know that all Canadians are grateful for your service.

A couple of days after that, announcing more "emergency measures," he said[102] truckers and medical staff and delivery workers "are keeping the country running … [and] deserve our thanks for everything they do."

Then just a few days after that, announcing the government subsidy for people put out of work by lockdowns, he specifically thanked truck drivers[103], along with other workers, who were "working day and night so that we can eat and take our medication."

---

101 https://pm.gc.ca/en/news/speeches/2020/03/22/prime-ministers-remarks-updating-canadians-and-thanking-them-helping-fight

102 https://pm.gc.ca/en/news/speeches/2020/03/24/prime-ministers-remarks-updating-canadians-measures-respond-covid-19

103 https://pm.gc.ca/en/news/speeches/2020/04/01/prime-ministers-remarks-updating-canadians-rollout-canada-emergency

And in a public address shortly after that, he named truck drivers again[104] as among the workers "doing more than their part… making sacrifices so the rest of the population can stay home."

In an address on Easter Weekend 2020[105], he even compared truckers to the Canadian soldiers who fought at Vimy Ridge to "defend the values we hold dear." He said of the soldiers, "their bravery and courage live on…in our truckers, cashiers, and all front line workers." Trudeau was being melodramatic, as usual. That's what drama teachers do. But everyone listening understood that there was some truth behind what he was saying: While the privileged laptop class was COVID-cocooning in their living rooms, enjoying their work-from-home quality time, truckers were out there in the world, bringing all of us the things we needed to survive, from groceries to gasoline to medical necessities.

A few months later, on Labour Day, Trudeau praised the truckers again.[106] "On this Labour Day, all Canadians owe a debt of gratitude to our workers – from those on the front lines to those who stayed home to keep others safe. To our truckers, rail, and port workers that kept our supply chains moving – we thank you."

It seemed that, for a while there, Justin Trudeau couldn't say enough good things about the truckers.

But then something changed. By 2021, political leaders like Trudeau were getting intoxicated with how much power they could give themselves, and how much they could take away from individual citizens. The media were cheering them on. The public was telling pollsters to punish dissenters harder and faster. People who once stood

---

104 https://pm.gc.ca/en/videos/2020/04/06/remarks-cerb-and-additional-measures-fight-economic-impacts-covid-19

105 https://pm.gc.ca/en/videos/2020/04/12/covid-19-pandemic-challenge-our-generation

106 https://pm.gc.ca/en/news/statements/2020/09/07/statement-prime-minister-labour-day

on their balconies banging pots and pans to thank their local nurses[107] were now braying for unvaccinated nurses to be fired.

Trudeau had every reason to believe that he could go after the truckers. That he did so was no surprise. What was surprising — what was *amazing* — was how the truckers stood their ground and fought back, and finally broke the momentum of our country's, and even the world's, seemingly endless march toward public-health tyranny.

To understand why, it helps to understand truckers.

One important thing to know about truckers is that they are justifiably proud people. They are also fiercely independent people. When they get behind the wheel, they are in control of tens of thousands of pounds of steel and cargo. They are road warriors who have to drive even when it's raining or snowing or hailing. If they call in sick, they don't get paid. If they need a break, they can't just ask a co-worker to fill in for them. If they screw up, it's on them; there's no one else to shift the blame to. These folks eat, breathe and live personal responsibility in a way that most people can't even imagine.

And many of them work punishing hours, away from home days or weeks at a time, sleeping in their own cabs, all while keeping to tight delivery schedules. It's damned hard work. It's also damned important work keeping our economy moving. And they have a right to be damned proud of it.

On November 19, 2021, the Trudeau government announced[108] that it was bringing the vaccine mandate to truckers. Look closely at the language they used in the announcement, because it's important.

"The Government of Canada is also announcing that as of January 15, 2022, certain groups of travellers, who are currently exempt from entry requirements, will only be allowed to enter the country if they

107 https://www.youtube.com/watch?v=sG8pcgOTYD4

108 https://www.canada.ca/en/public-health/news/2021/11/government-of-canada-announces-adjustments-to-canadas-border-measures.html

are fully vaccinated with one of the vaccines approved for entry into Canada."

This wasn't like previous mandatory vaccine orders, like for medical staff and public servants. Those workers weren't given an exemption. But the truckers had been given one. When the federal government issued its first order against "non-essential" international travel in March 2020, an explicit exception was made for truck drivers[109], as well as crews working in air and marine transport. We needed them to keep them to keep the economy going, to keep medical supplies and pharmaceuticals and food getting into Canada and distributed across the country. Keeping the trucks moving was the exact definition of essential. It was a matter of survival.

In February 2021, Trudeau announced strict new border measures[110]: Anyone coming into Canada would have to show a negative PCR test for COVID and they would still have to quarantine for 14 days, or risk "heavy fines and possible jail time." Trudeau called them some of the "strongest border measures in the world."

But he also said, once again, that there needed to be exceptions made for "essential travel, such as for truck drivers". Just like in March 2020, the reasons seemed obvious. The key word is "essential." That's why the exemption for truckers had always been completely uncontroversial: they were essential.

Absolutely nobody was clamouring for truckers to have to observe the same travel restrictions as everyone else. The travel restrictions themselves didn't even make any sense to begin with[111]: among other reasons, the PCR tests that required people to test negative can give positive results for weeks, or even months, after someone recovers from

---

109 https://pm.gc.ca/en/news/speeches/2021/02/12/prime-ministers-remarks-updating-canadians-covid-19-variants-vaccines-and

110 https://pm.gc.ca/en/news/speeches/2021/02/12/prime-ministers-remarks-updating-canadians-covid-19-variants-vaccines-and

111 https://www.theglobeandmail.com/opinion/article-canadas-current-travel-restrictions-dont-make-sense/

COVID. And Ottawa's draconian 14-day quarantine contradicted the rule in provinces that five days was enough to recover. Health officials didn't really understand COVID very well and they were mostly making these numbers up. The rules were pointless anyways. Viruses always find ways to cross international borders. Every country in the world, even tiny island states, eventually got COVID.

(Technically Turkmenistan still claims[112] it never had a single case, despite the fact that it has more than five million people and borders three countries. But the totalitarian government also makes it illegal for anyone to discuss the pandemic or even say the word "coronavirus." No one takes their impossible claim seriously.)

Even the most paranoid politicians knew that truckers were critical to keep what was left of the economy moving amid widespread lockdowns and border closures. That's why they kept thanking and praising the truckers. That's why truckers, unlike most other people, were also permitted to travel[113] in and out of the infamous "Atlantic bubble." That was when Nova Scotia, New Brunswick, Newfoundland and Prince Edward Island walled themselves off from the rest of Canada, making it virtually impossible for anyone to go in or out, attempting to mimic the doomed "COVID-zero" strategies used by China and Australia.

Plus, there was the fact that a trucker's workplace isn't like anyone else's. Truckers work, eat and sleep inside their trucks. They're all by themselves every day they're on the road. They're not exactly going to be easily catching or spreading COVID, regardless of whether they crossed a border or not.

That's why when Ottawa announced in August 2021 that it would start allowing regular travel again across the U.S.–Canada

---

112 https://en.wikipedia.org/wiki/COVID-19_pandemic_in_Turkmenistan

113 https://halifax.citynews.ca/coronavirus-covid-19-local-news/trucking-association-says-drivers-continue-to-face-long-waits-crossing-provincial-border-2552418

border for vaccinated people, it still maintained its exemption for truckers. Worrying about whether truckers were vaccinated, given how important they were and how little risk there was of them transmitting anything that wasn't already getting in much more easily, seemed utterly pointless. Besides, the vaccination rate for truckers was high anyway[114], about the same as for the Canadian population at large, at around 85 to 90 per cent.

So Trudeau's decision to suddenly announce in November 2021 that he would start punishing unvaccinated truckers by making it impossible to cross the border unless they were willing to immediately quarantine for weeks — robbing them of the ability to do their jobs and make their living — was yet another arbitrary rule that had no legitimacy in science or logic.

Trucking groups in Canada and the U.S. called it out for the madness that it was. The Canadian Trucking Alliance (CTA) said it "could spell even more trouble for the North American supply chain that is already facing challenges associated with the driver shortage." The industry was already grappling with a severe shortage of drivers, with 18,000 open vacancies, according to the CTA, "placing immense pressure on an already fragile national supply chain which is struggling to meet current demand." The CTA warned that Trudeau's decision wouldn't just affect the 10 or 15 per cent of unvaccinated Canadian truckers, but that as many as 40 per cent of American truckers would be banned from delivering goods to Canada. Both countries rely on billions of dollars of trade moving across the border every day. The whole system would break down.

When Trudeau decided to go to war against truckers, supply-chain shortages were already out of control. In October 2021 in the U.S., there were two billion out-of-stock messages for online shoppers

114 https://www.bbc.com/news/world-us-canada-60164561

alone, according to one study.[115] In November 2021, new moms were feeling a rapidly growing baby formula shortage, with 11 per cent of popular brands already out of stock.[116] Canadians were seeing more and more empty shelves at their supermarkets.[117] And the supply-chain bottlenecks were fuelling price increases in Canada[118], and inflation was growing faster than it had in nearly 20 years.[119]

The Liberals' irrational, unscientific, entirely political decision to attack truck drivers wasn't just going to punish the truckers. It was going to hurt every single person across Canada, with people least equipped to manage the supply-chain disruptions, poor and vulnerable people, set to suffer the most.

Things had clearly gone way too far. What kind of country had Canada become? We had governments who seemed far more obsessed with promoting vaccines and pushing up the stock prices of Pfizer and Moderna than they did with the reality and the struggles of the Canadian people.

Someone had to stop it. And the first person to say enough is enough was Brigitte Belton.

I will always admire Brigitte for what she did. She and I would become allies, although eventually she turned against me and the other Freedom Convoy organizers. Actually, she was determined to help throw me in jail, which is something I'll get into more a bit later. But Brigitte deserves 100-per-cent credit for the stand that she took. It was brave. And it was beautiful. And it was the beginning of a revolution.

---

115 https://blog.adobe.com/en/publish/2021/11/09/adobe-shoppers-have-seen-over-2-billion-out-of-stock-messages-online-october-2021

116 https://www.usatoday.com/story/money/2022/05/13/baby-formula-shortage-price-gouge-cost/9750034002/?gnt-cfr=1

117 https://dailyhive.com/vancouver/empty-grocery-stores-food-supply-food-shortage

118 https://www.bankofcanada.ca/2021/12/keeping-our-eyes-on-inflation/

119 https://www150.statcan.gc.ca/n1/daily-quotidien/211117/dq211117a-eng.htm

Brigitte is a trucker from Wallaceburg, Ont., just an hour from the U.S.-Canada border crossing at Windsor and Detroitt, so she was frequently driving back and forth between the two countries. She would always roll up at the border officer's booth not wearing a mask; she was exempted because she's asthmatic and has psychological trauma as a survivor of domestic abuse that is triggered by having her mouth covered. She'd never had a problem: the guards might ask her to put on a plastic shield, or they were understanding about it. She was up high in her truck with the window open. They were standing outside, down on the ground, in their booth. The risks were ridiculously low.

But when she pulled up to the Canadian border on November 16, 2021, the mood in the country was getting very dark. It was just three days before the Liberals announced they would be targeting cross-border truckers. They had just won an election a few weeks earlier that was all about scapegoating people who didn't co-operate with official pandemic orders, and promising to persecute them further.

The cruelty was clearly trickling down to the officials enforcing the orders. And so on that particular day, the border guard, for the first time, ordered Brigitte to put on a mask, or she could be arrested. She refused. They detained her in a secondary screening area and threatened her again with arrest. She refused.

Eventually they let her go with a warning. As she explained in a TikTok video she made afterward, she said she'd had enough. She wasn't going to get vaccinated, so the mandates threatened to end her career and financially ruin her. She was distraught and desperate, but resolute. "I don't know what I'm going to do next," she said.

As it happened, a few provinces away in Saskatchewan, Chris Barber was thinking about just that. Like Brigitte, Chris was an active TikTok user. Actually, that's an absolutely massive understatement. A lot of truckers are pretty active on TikTok. You'd probably be surprised how popular it is with truckers. But Chris is the TikTok king. His TikTok videos, which he posted under the handle BigRed1975, have racked up tens of millions of views. He's opinionated, he's funny, and he loves to troll people. He's probably the world's most epic troll.

Chris had also been making a whole lot of videos about the stupidity of the COVID restrictions. His videos were hugely popular among independent-minded truckers who had no time for the authoritarian nanny state that treated people like subjects to be controlled. Truckers like Chris were already upset about Ottawa's push for the trucking industry to adopt electronic logs, or e-logs, essentially tracking devices that provide records for the federal government to monitor the movements of truckers: where they go, where they eat, where they sleep, and even where they stop to use the bathroom.

But after the Trudeau government announced the vaccine mandate for truckers, you could sense from Chris's videos that his anger had reached a new level. He was furious and he used his TikTok platform to let the world know it. He quickly became the voice of truckers across Canada who felt betrayed by politicians who had once celebrated them as heroes, but were suddenly turning on them, attacking them, trying to make an example out of them in their militant war on the unvaccinated.

Brigitte was one of the thousands of truckers who had been watching Chris's videos on TikTok. And his anger was her anger, too. She got in touch with him and the two of them started talking about what they could do. Brigitte wanted to do a nationwide convoy trucker protest, full of horn honking and slow rolls tying up traffic across the country and backing up border crossings. She figured one day full of inconvenience would probably be enough to get Canadians and their leaders to remember how much they needed truck drivers, and put enough pressure on Ottawa to back off the pointless vaccine mandate.

I want to pause here to discuss the supposed U.S. vaccine mandate for truckers. A lot of people tried telling Canadian truckers and their supporters that our protesting didn't matter, because President Joe Biden had said he was going to start requiring cross-border truckers to be vaccinated, too. They said it didn't matter what Trudeau did, because unvaccinated Canadian drivers wouldn't be able to drive into the U.S., anyway. Let me be clear: those people have no clue what they were talking about.

First of all, the Biden rule was a choice between vaccines or testing[120], while Trudeau's order made vaccines the only option. Second of all, the Biden administration order only applied to businesses with 100 or more workers, so not independent contract drivers. And third of all[121], it exempted any workers "who do not report to a workplace where other individuals such as coworkers or customers are present." Biden's Department of Labor had made it clear that the vast majority of truck drivers would continue to be exempt from vaccine mandates. "Because they're driving a truck, they're in a cab, they're by themselves, they wouldn't be covered by this," U.S. Labor Secretary Marty Walsh said on November 4, 2021.[122]

Oh, and fourth of all, the U.S. Supreme Court blocked Biden's vaccine mandates a few weeks later[123], well before the Canadian protests against Trudeau's trucker mandates started. So, no, Biden's rule was not the problem. Trudeau's militancy went way beyond anything the U.S. was proposing. Canadian truckers would not have been put out of work by Joe Biden. Canada was the outlier. Even as business groups across the country, including the Canadian Chamber of Commerce and the Canadian Manufacturing Coalition, urged Ottawa to back down, and challenged the Liberals to produce any evidence truckers were a source of COVID spread, Trudeau stubbornly dug in and refused to reconsider.

---

120 https://www.whitehouse.gov/briefing-room/statements-releases/2021/11/04/fact-sheet-biden-administration-announces-details-of-two-major-vaccination-policies/

121 https://www.cnbc.com/2021/11/05/labor-secretary-says-most-truck-drivers-are-exempt-from-covid-mandate-handing-industry-a-win-.html

122 https://www.bloomberg.com/news/articles/2022-01-13/supreme-court-halts-osha-rule-that-covered-80-million-workers

123 https://www.bloomberg.com/news/articles/2022-01-13/supreme-court-halts-osha-rule-that-covered-80-million-workers

I am certain there were lots of truckers across Canada who were thinking that something had to be done to stand up to Trudeau. I was watching the anger growing on social media, and I was hearing about it from people that I knew from the Yellow Vest protests and United We Roll.

The first I heard about the national work stoppage that Chris and Brigitte were working on was when a friend of mine — Cindy Parker, who I met during the Yellow Vest demonstrations — messaged me the TikTok video that Chris had made.

"When is enough enough?" Chris said. "Twenty-third of January, let's say 12 noon wherever you are, shut the trucks down."

I asked Cindy what she thought about the whole convoy idea, because I didn't think the United We Roll convoy really made any difference or had much impact. And I asked some other friends, and they were all pretty pessimistic, too. But Glen Carritt, the guy who I mentioned was the organizer for the United We Roll convoy, gave me Chris's phone number and told me to call him.

In the meantime, James Bauder, who had driven from Alberta to Ottawa in the fall of 2021 to lead a small and largely unnoticed "Canada Unity" anti-mandate, anti-vaccine protest, was talking to Chris and Brigitte. James wanted them to think bigger than a one-day traffic jam: that there needed to be a full-on trucker convoy to Parliament Hill, where it would park right outside Justin Trudeau's office and right where the federal politicians and bureaucrats worked. That would put real pressure on them to end their insane war on the unvaxxed and lift their stupid, unscientific mandates.

I called Chris, the day after Cindy sent me his TikTok video. It turned out Chris and I had lived in the same part of Saskatchewan, when I was in Shaunavon, because he's from Swift Current, but we had never met before. By the time I spoke to him that day, James had convinced him and Brigitte that what was really needed was a convoy of trucks driving all the way to Ottawa, to bring the power of the people to Parliament Hill.

I don't know how it happened, since I was pretty skeptical of the idea. But by the time I'd hung up the phone with Chris, I was ready to help make it happen.

I had no idea what I was getting myself into.

CHAPTER 4:

THE FIGHT BEGINS

I had never planned to become the leader of anything.

I'm still not completely sure how it happened that I became the face of a Freedom Convoy that, at the beginning, I wasn't even sure was a very good idea. Even after that phone call with Chris, where he convinced me to help out, I probably didn't have a lot of confidence in my heart of hearts that the convoy would amount to much. I'm not a trucker, so it's not like I could just call up all my trucker friends and say "let's go do a convoy," so I had no idea whether truckers would even be up for it, other than Chris and Brigitte.

With no idea if it would be viable or not, I suppose I agreed to help anyway because I believed in the rightness of the cause, and it's in my nature to want to help out people who I think are on the wrong side of an injustice. And I guess doing something at least felt better than doing nothing.

We had come up with our plan by January 13, and we decided that January 23, the day that Chris had first proposed for his nationwide shutdown idea, would now be the day we'd start our convoy to Ottawa. We had given ourselves all of 10 days to pull it all together. We must have been out of our minds.

At first, I didn't know how involved I'd be. I certainly never expected to find myself trying to figure out what to do with millions of dollars in donations. Or meeting hundreds of people from across the country who just wanted to talk to me and share their experience. Or becoming the most visible spokesperson for a national movement of thousands. Or ending up arrested and held as a political prisoner for weeks in jail.

I had just offered to help Chris set up a Facebook and Twitter account and a fundraising page for the convoy.

I had some experience with running social media for the Yellow Vest protests and also doing some of the organizing. The first thing I did was set up some email and social media accounts, using the name: "Taking Back Our Freedoms Convoy." I remember I had heard someone use that expression, "taking back our freedoms," and I thought it was a great name.

As it turns out, it wasn't.

For one thing, we soon found out there was already another group called Taking Back Our Freedoms, which was against the vaccine mandate, and also pretty heavy on the anti-vaccine, pro-Ivermectin stuff. They focus a lot more on the medical issues, working with Dr. Paul Alexander, who worked with the Trump administration trying to promote herd immunity, and Rodger Hodkinson, the veteran pathologist who had been fighting against the hysteria, alarmism and fear around COVID, and the silencing of independent medical opinions.

Anyway, someone from that group got in touch with me within a couple of days and told me I couldn't use that name. I remembered that we had made the same mistake when I was organizing a local convoy in 2018, and someone called us and was just screaming at us because we had used their name, so I was very sensitive to the fact that I didn't want to be using another organization's name.

So I quickly renamed it the Freedom Convoy, just as a placeholder at first. But it ended up sticking. And it clearly turned out to be a much better name. Mainly because it's much catchier, but as a brand I think it's much less confrontational, which probably helped with the success of the convoy and also provided us the right direction for the spirit of the protest.

I think "taking back our freedoms" might have scared some people off who might have been worried that it was all about anger and fighting. Obviously we had a lot of people who were angry, and a lot of people who were very much ready to take a stand for their rights. But the success of the protest had so much to do with how it also drew in people who were just tired of the pandemic, and sad because of what the government had done to them. So many people were dispirited and hopeless, and it made them feel welcome and gave them hope again. I'm not sure if they would have joined us if we had called it "Taking Back Our Freedoms."

And the feeling as we met people driving across the country and the atmosphere when we got to Ottawa definitely felt more like a celebration of Canadian freedoms than a fight. As everyone saw, the people who were in a fighting mood in Ottawa weren't the protesters but the angry and paranoid Trudeau Liberals.

The funny thing is, once we were in Ottawa, the actual group that was called Taking Back Our Freedoms, whose name I accidentally almost used, actually showed up to try to take over the leadership of the convoy, after all. They kept coming into our leadership meetings and trying to dominate and control the decision-making, until we finally told them to stop. Eventually, they resorted to relocating their people to hotel rooms next to mine so they could keep constant watch on who was coming and going and what we were up to. They were actually peeking out every time they heard my door open, to see what was going on.

So, in retrospect, I think the name Freedom Convoy ended up being a brilliant name. And the way it happened, entirely accidentally, was the first thing that seemed to happen because someone, somewhere was guiding us in the right direction. As you'll soon find out, there were many, many things that seemed to happen because of providence, each one making us more and more certain that we were travelling a righteous path.

After I set up the Twitter and Facebook accounts, and the email addresses and all that, I began to set up a crowdfunding account with *GoFundMe*, which would let our supporters donate money to help with the expenses of the convoy, like fuel and food. The way it works is that *GoFundMe* asks you to set a target amount that you want to raise. You want to make it reasonable enough that people feel their donations, however small, will make a difference and help you get to your goal. So you don't want to set it unrealistically high.

I remember asking Chris what he thought we should set the target at, and he said he figured we could use around $250,000 to help provide for the truckers headed to Ottawa. I thought he was nuts! I said no way. I thought it was so impossible that we'd raise that much that we'd just look foolish and maybe even greedy. So I decided to set it at $100,000. Even that seemed high to me. I thought maybe we'd raise $20,000.

Because I thought we would only raise a bit, I made a big mistake by just linking the *GoFundMe* funds to a savings account that I had, but hadn't really been using. The account was completely busted after I had lost all my savings just trying to stay afloat during the lockdowns. In fact, it was 13 cents overdrawn. So I deposited 13 cents, to bring the balance up to zero before we even began fundraising the first dollar, so that no one could say I benefited even a few cents from the donations.

Suddenly, everything started happening very, very fast. It was incredible. The money started pouring in. Our Facebook page was inundated with messages from all across the country. People wanting to know how they could join us, or how they could help, or just to thank us for what we're doing.

The funds were growing by the thousands. By January 17, we had already broken through $100,000. As fast as we raised the *GoFundMe* targets — to $200,000, $300,000, $500,000 — donors would keep giving more. Eventually, *GoFundMe* said it couldn't release so much money into my personal account, which was probably for the best. So at one point, Chris and I finally set up a separate account, just for the convoy. And of course it wouldn't be long before that account was frozen by the government and the courts.

All the donations, all the well-wishers, all of it was breaking down my early skepticism about whether this would achieve anything more than the Yellow Vest protests or the United We Roll convoy. But the day that really made me realize the significance of what we were doing was the day I spoke to Noeline Villebrun, a clan mother and former chief from the Copper Dene First Nation in Yellowknife, all the way up in the Northwest Territories. We connected through a First Nations supporter who knew we needed to meet. And he was right. I didn't know it yet, but we really needed Noeline. And something out there made sure she was there for us.

On that first phone call, she wanted to tell me how much she supported the Freedom Convoy, and that she was going to do everything she could to help us. She said she would be contacting chiefs from tribes that she had connections with all across the country. She was also going to organize drummers to come and meet us along the way to Ottawa to drum in support of us. And she was also going to pray for us.

It's so hard to express in words how much that call meant to me. I couldn't stop myself from crying. It made me understand the importance of what we were trying to do in a far more meaningful way than I had ever thought about it before. Now hit me on a deep, heartfelt level.

Obviously the convoy had always seemed to me to be a just cause, but when I spoke to Noeline, I understood it was so much more than about fighting against vaccine mandates. We were reuniting a people that had been torn apart. Here I was connecting with a Dene clan mother all the way out in the territories. Our message was reaching her, and she was reaching out to us. It made me understand what this was really about. This was about humanity.

We had just been through two years of politicians and health officials and the police and the media trying to divide us all. They had tried to turn Canadians against Canadians. They had banned us from seeing each other, locking up our places of worship, outlawing sports and clubs and dancing, and ordering us not to even visit our friends and families. They encouraged us to be suspicious of one another, with snitch lines, and taught us to call each other murderers, and to scapegoat each other. They had tried to turn Canada into an ugly, angry, unforgiving and untrusting nation. They hadn't just dehumanized the unvaccinated. They had dehumanized us all.

I decided to make a Facebook Live video to broadcast from the Freedom Convoy Facebook page and tell people about my call with Noeline. I was already thinking that we needed to start communicating with people on a larger scale. I wanted our donors to know who I was, and how they could help out if they wanted to. I also wanted to be able to make our donors feel 100-per-cent reassured that we were going to be handling their money responsibly, and that everything would be handled in a completely transparent and accountable manner.

On January 18, 2022, I did my first Facebook Live broadcast, and said those eight fateful words that would set me off on an unintentional, accidental, entirely unpredictable path to fame .

"I'm Tamara, nice to meet all of you."

I talked about that amazing conversation I'd had with Noeline. It was just a two-minute video, but less than halfway in I was already choking up about it. I was so elated and touched over the incredible sense of unity I was feeling. "I am overwhelmed," I said. "Now is our time and we're going to do this and I just want to let you all know how much I appreciate you, all of us appreciate you. We are working our butts off to make this happen, but this isn't just about the organizers, this is about all of you. This is about all of us coming together and we will stand in solidarity."

We were just five days away from our scheduled departure of January 23, and all of the organizers were working around the clock trying to scramble to get things together. As I would tell our supporters in my next Facebook Live video, I was running on very little sleep, a lot of hopes and dreams, and a little bit of caffeine. But somehow, miraculously, we were being inundated with offers from people all across Canada to provide us with everything we needed, and more. People were offering us places to sleep along the way. They were offering us coffee stations, cases of water and donated food. More and more people were telling us they were going to join us, and drive to Ottawa with us. And the money just kept rolling in.

I decided then that we needed to have a finance committee, which I asked Noeline to help with, because she had experience with governance, having served as a chief of her First Nation. As I said, she and I would end up working together, and it started our wonderful friendship. Cindy Parker, who had first sent me Chris's TikTok video, agreed to help out on the committee as well. And we had a couple of bookkeepers, and an accountant who agreed to work as an advisor and help us when it came to start dispersing the funds, as well as to help us to stay in compliance with *GoFundMe*.

As the size of the donations kept growing into the hundreds of thousands of dollars, and eventually millions, *GoFundMe* was sending me regular emails, asking more and more questions. And they released the first million dollars to us, praising us for our "clear distribution plan" and because we "confirmed funds would be used only for participants who traveled to Ottawa to participate in a peaceful protest." We were keeping everything on the up and up.

But the questions from *GoFundMe* kept coming. One day it we would get three questions, then another five questions would arrive in my inbox the next day, and then I would get seven more questions the day after that. It seemed to never stop.

First it was, how are you going to disperse these funds? And what specifically are these funds for? I had already spelled out all of that right in the description I had written on the Freedom Convoy donation page: the money will be for travel expenses for the truckers to cover their cost of fuel to attend a peaceful protest in Ottawa.

But *GoFundMe* kept asking me to keep going over things we'd already told them. "Please confirm that funds raised will only go to reimburse the fuel costs of convoy participants," they wrote in one email. Then "Do you plan on posting an update to the fundraiser to reiterate that protests should remain peaceful, you do not condone any acts or threats of violence and that individuals suspected of engaging in illegal activity during the protests will not be eligible to receive funds?"

Then, "How much of the initial $1M of transferred funds has been distributed to participants and to how many participants?" And the more questions I answered, the more the questions kept coming.

At first, I naively thought *GoFundMe* was just doing their due diligence. But by the time we got to Ottawa, they were under so much pressure from the Trudeau government, the media and everyone else who was against us, that I quickly figured out that they were giving us the runaround and looking for some way to trip us up and cut us off. People were actually emailing them, saying that we were a terrorist organization and that they should shut us down, or that we were just a big fraud. The Ottawa police had admitted[124] that they had been lobbying *GoFundMe* to try to shut us down. So we now live in a country where police think they can decide, and enforce, who can raise money and who can't.

I knew there was no way that *GoFundMe* had given this much of a hard time to *GoFundMe* campaigns for Black Lives Matter, or for the Capital Hill Autonomous Zone (CHAZ) anti-police anarchists who took over downtown Seattle in 2020 and burned down businesses, and

124 https://thepostmillennial.com/ottawa-police-admit-to-lobbying-gofundme-to-withhold-funds-from-canadian-truckers

permitted shootings, rapes and robberies. *GoFundMe* kept providing funds for CHAZ[125] even after people were murdered there. *GoFundMe* even tweeted support for the protesters[126], and encouraged people to donate.

Murders, robberies, shootings, arson and rapes were apparently not a violation of *GoFundMe*'s terms of service. But even after they couldn't find any problems with our transparency and bookkeeping, once we got to Ottawa they just went ahead and announced that we had somehow violated their service terms, citing "police reports of violence and other unlawful activity,"[127] which was just a lie. Not one single person had ever been hurt and not a single building had been damaged by our people.

And of course the Ottawa police not only thanked them for cutting us off, but tried warning any other crowdfunding sites not to help us either. "The decision to withhold funding for these unlawful demonstrations is an important step and we call on all crowdfunding sites to follow," the Ottawa police posted on their Twitter account.[128] So now the police were also deciding what kind of demonstrations were "unlawful."

GoFundMe actually tried to steal our supporters' money. When they cut us off, they said that people had a limited time to request a refund directly[129], because apparently they couldn't just refund everyone's money automatically. After that, the site was just going to redistribute any remaining funds to unnamed "credible and established charities." When Ron DeSantis, the Florida governor, heard about

---

125 https://thepostmillennial.com/gofundme-chaz-chop-murder

126 https://twitter.com/JackPosobiec/status/1489777007382745094?ref_

127 https://www.dailymail.co.uk/news/article-10478989/GoFundMe-cancels-Freedom-Convoy-distribute-9M-donations-charities.html

128 https://twitter.com/OttawaPolice/status/1489754844097392640?ref_

129 https://www.dailymail.co.uk/news/article-10478989/GoFundMe-cancels-Freedom-Convoy-distribute-9M-donations-charities.html

that, he called it a "fraud" and "deceptive"[130] and announced that he was going to have his attorney general investigate it. That immediately got *GoFundMe* to backtrack on its "redistribution" plan[131], that would have seen our money go to Black Lives Matter or Extinction Rebellion or whatever other radical causes they wanted to give it to.

Well that sure scared them straight. They announced that they were suddenly able to refund the money to donors, automatically, after all. Amazing how they figured it out all out right after DeSantis threatened to investigate them. But I think they still need to be investigated. Left-wing Silicon Valley billionaires already control what we can say on Facebook, Twitter and YouTube. *GoFundMe* is just another way for them to control which causes can raise money, and which ones can't.

It was a good thing we figured out early enough on that *GoFundMe* was trying to screw us, because that gave us time to set up another fundraising campaign with GiveSendGo, which is a free, Christian fundraising site that provides an alternative to the dominance of *GoFundMe*. The founders, Jacob Wells and his sister Heather Wilson, wanted to give people another option to raise funds online because *GoFundMe* was cancelling so many conservative campaigns that it considered too controversial. *GoFundMe* only allows controversial left-wing campaigns, like Black Lives Matter and CHAZ.

We launched our GiveSendGo campaign and were helped directly by Wells, the site's co-founder and CFO, and he was absolutely awesome.

Ontario Premier Doug Ford is probably one the most fanatical pro-lockdown, pro-mandate politicians outside of China. I mean, indoor dining in Toronto was shut down for an appalling 382 days[132] and kids in Ontario were out of school for a total of 28 weeks since March

---

130 https://twitter.com/govrondesantis/status/1489978237304426501?lang=en

131 https://www.foxbusiness.com/technology/gofundme-backtracks-canadian-trucker-money-fraud-investigation-threat

132 https://twitter.com/cfib/status/1405197538819465220

2020[133], which is thoroughly shameful. Needless to say, he was not a fan of our freedom movement and so he arranged for his provincial courts to issue a "restraining order" against GiveSendGo demanding the site freeze all of our funds.

The province's attorney general's office said the order would prohibit[134] "any person from disposing of, or otherwise dealing with, in any manner whatsoever, any and all monetary donations made through the Freedom Convoy 2022 and Adopt-a-Trucker campaign pages on the GiveSendGo online fundraising platform." Adopt-a-Trucker was a program that had been set up by Chris Garrah, one of our organizers, after we got to Ottawa. It allowed people to directly sponsor the living expenses of people who were staying in town for the protest.

When the Ontario government did that, Jacob Wells told Ontario to stuff it. The company said Ontario had no control over an American company, and that the site wasn't holding any of our funds, anyway. They had immediately transferred them all to the corporation we had set up to hold the funds.

"Know this! Canada has absolutely ZERO jurisdiction over how we manage our funds here at GiveSendGo," the company posted on its Twitter feed.[135] "All funds for EVERY campaign on GiveSendGo flow directly to the recipients of those campaigns, not least of which is The Freedom Convoy campaign.

I don't know for sure if Jacob Wells personally supported our cause, but I do know that his motivation for his work is very much all about not giving in to cancel culture. And I have nothing but respect for him and his organization.

133 https://theconversation.com/after-ontarios-covid-19-school-closures-a-responsive-recovery-plan-is-critical-177514

134 https://www.cnn.com/2022/02/11/business/givesendgo-trucker-convoy-protest/index.html

135 https://twitter.com/givesendgo/status/1491940399505682434?lang=en

On top of the avalanche of financial support and offers to help that we were getting before we even rolled out on our drive to Ottawa, we were also being completely overwhelmed by the messages coming through social media. We needed to set up a social media team to handle it all.

As soon as I saw how fast the momentum was gaining, I realized that we really needed to shift our communications focus to safety and to letting the public know that, we weren't going to be coming to Ottawa waving pitchforks and torches to rampage and pillage. We were just coming to peacefully protest.

I already knew that with the huge amount of support we were getting, we were bound to attract a few bad apples. I had seen that happen with the Yellow Vest movement, and how the media had gone trolling through comments[136] on Twitter and Facebook from any random people who said they supported our movement, and finding anything they could to call us "racist" or "terrorists" or a "hate group."

I knew from the start that the media would be gunning for us, because we were going against the government's narrative. As I said before, most of the media in this country no longer think their mission is to hold the government to account for the people, but to hold the people to account for the government. If we had been climate protesters coming to Ottawa, or Idle No More, or some kind of anti-racist convoy, I have no doubt the CBC and The Globe and Mail and Toronto Star would have been drooling all over us, celebrating us as a marvellous example of grassroots empowerment. The Liberal government probably would have covered the expenses for Greta Thunberg to fly in to protest along with us. And chains wouldn't be able to hold back Trudeau from racing out to take a knee with us for a photo op.

Instead, they would be doing all they could to make our legitimate grassroots empowerment seem like a menace to society. And so I started

136 https://www.canadaland.com/far-right-yellow-vests-taking-over-canada/

early on making it very clear to all the organizers and to get the message out to all our supporters that this was a peaceful protest. If there was anyone acting in a threatening manner, or being aggressive or violent, we needed to be clear they did not represent us, and they weren't to be considered part of our movement, and that it needed to be reported to the police right away, or to let us know and we would report it to the police.

It would be similar advice that Brad Wall, the former premier of Saskatchewan, would give to Chris as we were heading out to Ottawa. I remember that the media went after him, too, because he had dared to speak to us anti-mandate deplorables. "Former Sask. premier Brad Wall gave strategic advice to key convoy organizer," was the headline that CTV ran in July 2022[137], after they got their hands on some of Chris's text messages that the cops had in evidence that I guess the government's attorneys were leaking to reporters. A bunch of other news outlets then followed the story[138], acting like this was some huge scandal.[139]

And what subversive and seditious "strategic advice" did Wall give to Chris?

"Your group will likely be provoked by counter protesters and it is so important that they don't take the bait," is what Wall texted. "Also it is really important that any of those who are trying to hitch their wagon to this convoy with ulterior motives and off messages — especially racist stuff be openly and roundly condemned by the organizers."

Evidence came out in public at the Emergencies Act inquiry that the Integrated Terrorism Assessment Centre and the Canadian Security

137 https://www.ctvnews.ca/politics/former-sask-premier-brad-wall-gave-strategic-advice-to-key-convoy-organizer-1.5973718

138 https://www.cbc.ca/news/canada/saskatchewan/sask-wall-convoy-1.6510945

139 https://thestarphoenix.com/news/saskatchewan/moe-says-he-didnt-know-wall-advised-sask-leader-of-convoy-protest

Intelligence Service (CSIS) had confirmed that we were advocating only peaceful protests. That we were urging our organizers, supporters and all truckers to follow the law. These government spy agencies were all over the protest once we got to Ottawa. They even had Canadian special forces in a military surveillance plane flying circles over our protest.[140] And they confirmed that we had actually succeeded in keeping far-right extremist organizations from infiltrating our group. Of course, none of this would end up stopping the Liberals, the NDP, the media, and everyone else against us from calling us terrorists, racists and hate-mongers. But it did make them seem awfully ridiculous when they did.

When I wasn't working hard to keep our messaging on track, I was also trying to put all the other logistics together just sitting at my kitchen table in front of my computer, with two monitors, working 14 or 16 hours every day. I had Google Maps open, and Facebook, and Twitter, and hundreds of emails coming in every day. (Not all of the messages coming in were friendly, mind you.) And my phone was ringing every few minutes, and I had to leave it plugged in or the battery would die.

Organizations and individuals were calling me with offers and inquiries on how to help or offering advice. Politicians were calling me to offer support. I was in constant communication with the finance team, the social media team, and the road captains. I was getting literally 50 to 100 phone calls each day, while I'm also calling Chris, and Brigitte is calling me, and other organizers are trying to get in touch, as well as all of the supporters and people wanting to offer supplies. And there are piles of scribbled notes to myself all over the place that no one can read but me. It was a disaster area.

Dwayne was a real champ through all of this. I am sure he was wondering where his wife went. He was great at making sure I was

---

140 https://ottawacitizen.com/news/national/defence-watch/surveillance-aircraft-over-ottawa-during-freedom-convoy-protest-operated-by-canadian-special-forces-dnd-confirms

eating and getting enough water, anything I needed he would make sure I had. I am sure we barely spoke during that time. If I wasn't at my computer or on the phone I was squeezing in as much sleep as I was able to. Although Dwayne isn't very political and didn't always understand what I was doing or why, he was incredibly supportive. He made suppers, ordered suppers, went on coffee runs, grocery runs, he essentially ran the household while I was glued to my computer.

The convoy logistics were becoming a victim of success. The more people that wanted to come with us to Ottawa, the more complicated the trip became. The trip was obviously going to take several days, and truckers can only drive so many hours before they are required to shut their trucks down for a break. We had to time out where there would be places for all our people to stop. And while the big-rig truckers could sleep in their cabs along the way, there were more and more people who wanted to join us in smaller trucks or cars. So we also needed to find hotel rooms for them, and not every town along the way would have a hotel or motel, and the ones who did, might not have enough rooms.

Then there were the people who wanted to donate food, coffee, blankets, or diesel exhaust fluid, important to trucks. And they all wanted us to stop in their communities, so we had to figure out how to co-ordinate a way to make a couple stops every day in these places. That way we could have a stretch, get something to eat, and most importantly, meet all these wonderful supporters, so many of whom wanted to share their stories of how they were suffering because of government pandemic orders. That was such an important part of the trip, because it reminded us every day what this was all about. The stories were so heartbreaking, but so meaningful, because we knew when we heard them that we were on the right side of history.

We also had to figure out where the different convoys, from the coast of B.C., and southern Alberta, and northern Saskatchewan, and Manitoba, and all the places that people were joining us from, could converge together along the way, so we could all roll into Ottawa together. But we also had to be mindful of leaving enough gaps on the highway, for other travellers, for safety. We even had to worry about the most minor details, like making sure everyone had enough washer fluid.

And, naturally, we would need a lot of fuel.

We had been planning to have fuel bulkers — the tanker trucks that deliver gasoline to your local gas station — arranged along the way to Ottawa, because were worried that just using truck stops or cardlocks would end up with bottlenecks if you had a bunch of trucks all lined up trying to fill up.

I had made a deal with Federated Co-op, based out of Saskatoon. It's the same group that runs the Co-op grocery stores in Western Canada, but they also have an oil refinery and run a big gas distribution and retail gas operation. They operate in every province from B.C. to Manitoba. And we came up with this great plan together: We had a route mapped out for the truckers that directed them to a Federated Co-op yard, and we were going to have the rigs file in by two rows, with a gap between them, and have the bulkers just be in the middle and fill trucks on both sides. Then the trucks in front would drive off, and then they'd fill the next two in line.

Once we had that deal in place, I wanted to let everyone know that we were grateful for their help, and so we posted a message online, with a big thank-you to Federated Co-op for working with us.

Then, shortly after that, I got a call from the company, and they were pulling out. They just said, sorry, we can't help you, after all. So obviously they were being pressured. It was the same tactic that people hostile to us would use on *GoFundMe* and any other companies that tried to do business with us.

Have you ever heard the old saying about protest movements, first they ignore you, then they attack you, and then they build monuments to you? Well, before we started rolling out to Ottawa, everyone seemed to be ignoring us. The media and the politicians either didn't care about us, or were hoping that if they didn't pay us any attention, that maybe we'd just disappear. Maybe they thought this would be like another United We Roll convoy, and that a couple of hundred angry Albertans would show up in Ottawa for a few speeches and a couple of protests, and that would be it. Maybe they thought we were just blowing smoke.

Now, after they came after Federated Co-op, I could tell that people weren't ignoring us anymore.

I could tell that now they were going to start fighting us.

CHAPTER 5:

'THANK YOU FOR SAVING OUR FUTURE'

One thing I know for sure: when it comes to crowds, Manitoba wins.

Don't get me wrong. As our convoy rolled across Canada, there were swarms of supporters, in the towns and on the roadsides and at the truck stops, waving and cheering at us from the overpasses. When our first trucks left from the West Coast on January 23, I had one of the ladies who was on my finance committee out there take a video on her phone and send it to me. Already there were people lined up on the side of the road, cheering and clapping and waving.

All of them, in every province, were wonderful and supportive. They came out and stood in the snow and the freezing weather and waited for hours. Some of them for five or six hours! I heard from parents all along the route who had pulled their children from school to come see us, recognizing the magnitude of this event for our country.

Most of the truckers joined us in Alberta and Saskatchewan, so by the time we got to Manitoba, there were so many trucks it could take over an hour for the whole convoy to pass. By the time we got close to Ottawa, there were even more that had come in from Quebec, Newfoundland, New Brunswick and Nova Scotia. By the time we rolled into the nation's capital on January 29, our convoy was an incredible 100 kilometres long.

Chris had driven out from Swift Current to pick me up in Alberta on January 24, so I could ride out with him most of the way. My parents took their own pilot truck, a pickup, and I'd sometimes sit with them for a few hours along the way, too.

No matter who I was riding with, though, I was tearing up nearly non-stop, from Alberta to Ottawa. Before this all started, I swear to God, I hadn't cried for a decade. I've just never been an emotional person. But now, I just couldn't stop. There were just so many hundreds of Canadians coming together to support us. I saw little old ladies on their knees on the side of the road praying for us. I saw little kids holding up signs that read "thank you for saving our future." It just got me every time. Especially kids and old people. Seeing them would hit me right in my emotional gut and instantly turn me into a puddle of tears.

But they also gave me so much of the strength I would soon need for all that was about to come.

In the days before we rolled out, as people were reaching out to us through email and phone and social media, I had heard so many tragic, awful stories already of the suffering people had endured during two years of government pandemic decrees. The first one I remember that really impacted me was this lady that sent a message to the Facebook page. She said she had a 12-year-old son with muscular dystrophy, and he wasn't allowed to go to the pool for his swimming therapy because he's not vaccinated, so his mobility was getting rapidly worse. I remember another lady messaged me that she had an autistic daughter, and one of the few things that brought her daughter joy in life was going out the movies, but she wasn't allowed to do even that, and the daughter couldn't understand why.

I heard from people who weren't able to visit their sick and dying parents locked up in long-term care facilities. People whose loved ones died afraid and alone. They had lost their jobs, their cars, their homes. Their brother, or husband had killed himself. It was just heart-wrenching. I tear up now, nearly a year later, just thinking about them all and everything they went through, and so much suffering that didn't need to happen.

When we got on the road, and I started meeting more of these people, face to face, when we would stop in communities along the way, my heart would break every time. I had been making Facebook Live videos for our Freedom Convoy page in the days before we left, and I was broadcasting updates from the road. I wanted to show the world all the trucks that were already rolling, and the huge and wonderful crowds that were coming out to cheer us on, and I guess I had pretty quickly become the recognizable face of the movement at this point.

So as soon as I'd step out of the truck at one of these stops, people would just come up to me and want to share their stories. Some would just grab me, and hug me, and sob on my shoulder. I remember one time, when I was riding with my parents in their pilot truck, as we were pulling into Brandon, Man., I had rolled the window down as we drove along the service road. We had parked for just a minute or two, and this woman standing on the side of the road saw me and immediately came running at top speed over to our truck, and I swear she grabbed me so hard in a hug through the window, she almost pulled me out of the truck window. She was just sobbing, telling me how she had lost her job, and lost pretty much everything she had, because of what had been done to her.

These are the stories I was hearing every day. Every single day. People would tell me they had been planning on killing themselves until the Freedom Convoy had given them hope. I talked to one father who had his whole family living in his car with him because he had lost his job, then they had lost their house, and they had almost nothing left.

These stories were all so painful and sad. But they were something else, too. They were a sign of resilience. They were a sign that none of us had lost our hope yet. These people who had come to cry with us, to talk with us, to pray with us, some of them drove for hours to be there. And they stood for hours to be there for us. It was minus-20 or minus-30 degrees on the Prairies and in Ontario. Canadians were showing that they had not been beaten yet. They were proof that the cold weather, and the cold, cruel and ruthless face of the government "public health" bureaucracy, was still no match for the warmth of our humanity and our support and love for one another.

When Chris and I set out on the road, we were obviously wowed by the crowds right away, but we figured it was mostly an Alberta-Saskatchewan phenomenon. We mistakenly thought that when we moved through Manitoba and Ontario, that the crowds would start to dwindle.

They didn't. The closer we got to Ottawa, the more people came out to cheer us, from the side of the highways, at the truck stops, and from the overpasses. They were lined up on lonely service roads, and at intersections, off-ramps and turnoffs. The CB radio would crackle with trucker voices telling us when we were about to pass another bunch. I would take videos of them as we drove past and broadcast them on Facebook Live so the whole world could see how many supporters were coming out for us. Chris would happily honk his thanks at them as we drove past.

But I will never forget Manitoba. I mean, having lived there, I know Manitoba is not a province that has been known in recent decades for being big into activism, unlike Alberta or Quebec. The rural areas tend to be more conservative, politically, and they vote that way, but the rest of the time, they busy themselves with ranching and farming and working, and they tend to behave themselves.

As I mentioned, when I lived there during the pandemic, I sensed a widespread obedience to the mask mandates, lockdowns and social distancing and all of it. But knowing Manitoba people, I think so many were just nervous about speaking out and vocally raising questions about the strange things they were being told, and the bizarre directives they were being ordered to follow. And I suppose when they heard about what we were doing, they knew they weren't alone — and that masses of people all around them had been waiting for someone to stand up and speak out, too.

It was as we were driving between Headingley, Man. and Winnipeg that I looked out the window, and, man, it was just the most beautiful, most perfectly Canadian, most wonderfully human sight I have ever witnessed. It truly made me fall deeply in love with this great country of ours.

It was the biggest crowd we had seen the entire way out. There were thousands of people. But it wasn't just the incredible numbers. It was who they were, and what they represented. There were First Nations people dressed in their full regalia, beating on their drums and dancing. And beside them were a group of Hutterite women, holding signs and clapping for us. And next to them there was a group of Sikh guys who were just hopping and whooping and hollering. And then there were nuns — in full habits — and they're holding up signs, and cheering for us, too. There were kids, and adults, and old people. It was like all of us were there, all of Canada, gathered there together, on the side of the road.

It was truly a miraculous sight to behold. And watching all that, and with me laughing, and crying of course, I had this incredible epiphany that this whole story we're always being told about Canada being divided, and regions being against each other, and politics being polarized, it just wasn't true. It didn't matter what god you worshipped, what colour your skin was, what part of the country you lived in, who you followed or supported as a political party.

I remember there were these snowmobilers, too, who were racing us up and down the ditch at the side of the road, and they had Canadian flags tied to hockey sticks standing up from the back of their sleds. I mean, a snowmobile with a hockey stick flying the Maple Leaf: you just can't get any more Canadian than that.

When we rolled into Winnipeg, there were about seven or eight Hutterite colonies around the area that had driven in from the country to bring just the biggest feast for us that I had ever seen. I mean, they had literal trailers filled with food. Everything from soup and sandwiches to entire roasts that they had made for us.

When we arrived at our planned stop I remember the police wouldn't let us all in, because the convoy had grown so long. These Hutterites fed around a thousand supporters there that evening and then packed up and followed us all the way to Kenora, Ont. They fed us there in the dark at about 10:30 at night, in minus-28-degree weather. The kindness and generosity of these people really know no bounds and we will be forever grateful to them.

In the five days we drove together from Alberta to Ottawa, it felt like Chris and I barely had time to speak with each other because one of us was always on the phone. Chris was over the moon because he was getting to talk to everyone from Brad Wall to Fox News in the U.S. At one point, I remember he was doing a live interview over the phone with Sean Hannity, and he had Tucker Carlson's production team on hold on the other line.

We were also staying in constant touch with police forces across the country. All of the police, until we got to Ottawa, had been just great. We had appointed road captains who were in charge of certain groups from different parts of Canada and it was their job to co-ordinate with law enforcement in their areas. We would give them advance notice that we were coming, where our stops and staging areas would be, and they were professional and helpful. Meanwhile, Chris and Pat King, who had sort of his own group of convoy followers, and some others, were calling ahead from Manitoba to the Ontario Provincial Police to get them ready for our arrival in Ontario.

As we rolled from Manitoba to Ontario, the crowds didn't get any smaller. There were still so many people along the roads and on the overpasses. At one point, some folks in the ditch off the shoulder of the road started setting off these big, beautiful fireworks over the highway as we drove under them. It felt like we were in a movie.

Meanwhile, the closer we got, and the bigger the crowds grew, the more money was pouring into our *GoFundMe* and other fundraising channels. It was hitting a rate of almost a million dollars every day. I kept having to raise our fundraising goal, because one of the girls from the finance committee would text me and say "we're almost at $5 million, you need to raise the target." And I'd raise it another million. And then another million. And every time I did, I would feel sicker and sicker to my stomach. It was so exciting, obviously, on one hand. But on the other hand, every time I did that, I would just get more nauseous. Because I knew that with all that money, some lawyers, somewhere would be trying to figure out a way to come and take it away from us. I was right about that.

The funny thing is, we barely touched any of it. The whole way out to Ottawa, I had truckers coming to me asking me for help paying for gas and other things. Even though the account was still in my name, I didn't have access to it, because the finance committee — which I had set up! — had made rules that every expense needed to be approved, and had to be backed up by receipts. I remember one of the bookkeepers thought I should stand at the gas pumps and write down every single tractor trailer and the driver's name and their licence plate number and how many litres they got, and collect the receipts. I told her that was absolutely not going to work, it wasn't even close to realistic.

We had so much money, and the finance committee would barely let me give any of it out. There were times when I was really frustrated about that, because I knew the drivers really needed it, but I just couldn't get the approvals. I had a few moments of anger when I would complain to Chris, "We have all this money and I can't do anything with it." But they were the professionals, so I knew I should listen to them.

I realize now that what the girls on the finance committee did was so smart. What they were doing was exactly the reason we had formed the committee in the first place. They were only looking out for me, for the convoy and for all of the donors. I admit I'm the first one who would have been handing out wads of cash to anyone who seemed like they needed it, because I don't like to see people in need. So, that could've landed me in a lot of trouble. I'm so proud of what they did and of their professionalism.

We ended up spending all of $26,000 in total — with every last cent of it accounted for. We had decided early on that whatever money we didn't need for ourselves, we would donate to Canadian veterans. But *GoFundMe* had only released the first million dollars before they caved in to the pressure from the government and police and cancelled our campaign, and ended up refunding the rest to donors.

We had raised about $10 million through GiveSendGo and approximately $400,000 through direct donations. But that's all frozen in an escrow account because a bunch of lawyers want to get their hands on it. One, an Ottawa lawyer named Paul Champ, has started a bizarre class-action lawsuit against our group on behalf of a group of Ottawa residents who claim they were traumatized by our presence. But he'll have to compete with the attorney general of Ontario, who also wants to seize the cash. The reality is we got there with no money, we stayed with no money, and we got home with no money. It was never really about the money anyway, but the statement *behind* the money. I'm proud to say that.

This whole time, we knew where we were going, but we didn't have a plan yet as to what we were going to do when we were there, which I guess was a pretty significant oversight on our part. Before we left, I honestly thought that we'd drive out there, stay there for about a week, and then come home, but it didn't quite turn out that way. There was no clear plan of attack for getting our message across as far as what we wanted to see achieved.

We had been entirely focused on the logistics of our arrival. For example, we had set up what we called our Ground Zero team, including Janet Seto and Chris Garrah. Chris Garrah was the one who had later set up the Adopt-a-Trucker fundraising campaign to help get money for fuel and food directly to the truckers, which was easier than getting that stuff from the main fundraising through the finance committee.

The Ground Zero team was getting the infrastructure ready for when we arrived, and I was obviously dealing with them quite a bit. Things like: how people were going to shower, where they were going to stay, how they were going to eat, where they could gather. They were the ones in charge of organizing the port-a-potties, too. They had also co-ordinated with some farmers outside the city who had offered their fields for us to park trucks outside the city.

We had all agreed that safety was our top priority. You wouldn't have known it from the news coverage, because they never mentioned it, but we always made sure lanes were open for emergency vehicles the whole time we were in Ottawa. In fact, it was the police who ended up blocking the streets: They were using snowplows, graders, cement barricades and police vehicles to block them so that more trucks couldn't come in, and then they blamed us for blocking traffic! In reality, when we got to Ottawa, we were planning on keeping the trucks outside the downtown. And that's where a lot of them ended up, anyway, including the farms around the city — I called them outposts, and there were at least five of them —because we needed to keep certain lanes open for safety reasons.

But as we moved nearer to our destination, it began to really hit me that we didn't know what would really be waiting for us when we got there. I knew for a fact that we weren't going to be allowed to succeed. Trudeau had already made it clear how much he detested us. "We know the way through this pandemic is to get everyone vaccinated,"[141] he lectured to the TV cameras the day before the protest. "The small, fringe minority of people who are on their way to Ottawa or who are holding unacceptable views that they're expressing, do not represent the views of Canadians."

141 https://www.youtube.com/watch?v=vDfMybczw1k

Trudeau had already decided we were a "fringe" with "unacceptable views" who, as he had said earlier, could not be "tolerated." We were not, in his opinion, Canadians. Even though there were thousands of us. Even though thousands of more had come out to greet us. Even though thousands more yet had donated to our cause. Of course, we knew these were real Canadians. The Native dancers. The Sikhs. The dudes on their snowmobiles. The Hutterites. The nuns. The families. The grandparents. The little kids. They were all so Canadian that my heart had nearly burst with pride and love for this great nation when I saw them.

It was a truth that was toxic to Trudeau. He needed the public to believe that a good Canadian was an obedient Canadian. Obedient to him and his government. Good Canadians got their injections. Good Canadians were those who stayed locked down and silently accepted their government handouts. Good Canadians agreed with him. Anyone else was unacceptable. Anyone else could not be tolerated.

And that narrative wasn't just Trudeau's. The same dogma was the driving force of governments around the world, from Ottawa and Washington to Moscow and Beijing. They all relied on the illusion that everyone agreed with their "science," by masquerading as consensus what was in reality a rigidly enforced cult of compliance.

It occurred to me that if that phoney façade crumbled in Canada, it would crumble everywhere. And there was a lot of great power invested in that narrative. I remember turning to Chris Barber in the cab of his truck as we barrelled toward Ottawa and saying we might be arrested. That we might even be shot.

Thankfully, I was wrong about getting shot. Unfortunately, I was all too right about us getting arrested.

And I was also right that what we were about to do in Ottawa would shake the world. We ended up inspiring convoys in dozens of countries: in the U.S.[142], across Europe[143], in South America[144], in Australia[145] and New Zealand[146]. Donald Trump said Canadian truckers were "doing more to defend American freedom than our own leaders by far."[147] Elon Musk tweeted that "Canadian truckers rule" and that based on our popular support, he said, "It would appear that the so-called 'fringe minority' is actually the government."[148]

While we knew going in that the political-medical control complex would be gunning for us, it wasn't long before we started to see other threats emerging all around us.

The size and success of the convoy even before we got to Ottawa had already unfortunately set off power struggles inside the movement. I shouldn't have been surprised that so many people wanted to jump in front of the parade. I know for some people, like Brigitte Belton, it was about getting the credit. Other people were thinking about the money. I want to believe that everyone who came with us was there for the right reasons, but once we had tens of thousands of supporters, millions of dollars, and Fox News and Elon Musk and Donald Trump in the mix, I think some people started to let their focus get compromised. People were always asking me for money. They wanted us to buy sound systems, or help them set up their own fundraising campaigns. When they saw me, they didn't see *me,* they saw millions of dollars over my head.

---

142 https://www.nbcnews.com/tech/internet/us-trucker-convoy-picks-momentum-foreign-meddling-adds-fray-rcna15932

143 https://www.washingtonpost.com/world/2022/02/10/europe-ban-freedom-convoy/

144 https://www.youtube.com/watch?v=1aFEar_5h68

145 https://www.washingtonpost.com/world/2022/02/08/australia-trucker-protest-canberra/

146 https://www.nbcnews.com/news/world/new-zealand-police-arrest-covid-truckers-canada-freedom-convoy-protest-rcna15667

147 https://www.youtube.com/watch?v=3yDtRxrNduc

148 https://twitter.com/elonmusk/status/1486772334635536395?lang=en

We were also starting to attract Canadian politicians. A bunch of candidates in the 2019 Conservative leadership race, including Peter MacKay, Leslyn Lewis and Derek Sloan, as well as Rick Peterson and Jim Karahalios, who had tried to run but didn't qualify. Later on, Candice Bergen, the acting leader of the Conservative party, wanted to do a photo op with us at an A&W fast-food restaurant far away from Parliament Hill for 10 minutes. It didn't impress me that she didn't actually want to be seen near the protest zone, so I took a pass on that. Leslyn Lewis later came down in person and had the integrity to meet the truckers face to face.

We had decided in a vote on a Zoom meeting before we departed for Ottawa that we needed to stay non-partisan. We wanted to make sure that we left the door open to any politician from any party to support us if they wanted. Maxime Bernier of the People's Party of Canada spent a lot of time at the protest. In fact, the PPC tried to take over one of our press conferences. We went in there, and all these party supporters were in there wearing PPC hats. We had to put a stop to that, because we didn't want to be seen as partisan, so we had them turn their hats around and stay quiet.

Pierre Poilievre, soon to be the leader of the Conservative party, met with us as well. So did Randy Hillier, who was sitting as an Independent in the Ontario legislature after Doug Ford kicked him out of the provincial Progressive Conservative caucus. Not a single member of the Trudeau Liberals, the elected government that supposedly represents all of Canada, showed up to even hear what we had to say, of course.

Some of the power struggles we faced were more petty than others. At one point we had made a wrong turn and were heading toward Sudbury, about five hours northwest of Ottawa, when one of our guys from Medicine Hat, we called him "Revvin' Kevin," kept trying to pass in front of everyone, so he could get to Ottawa first. It wasn't safe for him to keep pulling out and pulling back in. Remember, we were driving in the middle of January, when the roads can be dodgy at the best of times. Chris got into a big fight with Kevin telling him to knock it off, but he just wouldn't. And when we turned into Sudbury, I saw him break off and head off toward Ottawa, so he could get there first. It seemed like such a silly thing for him to get so obsessed about that he was willing to put people, and himself, in danger.

There was another group that also set up camp in Ottawa before we got there, at the intersection of Rideau Street and Sussex Drive, just a couple blocks east of the Parliament buildings, that came in from Quebec. They ended up being unusually difficult to deal with. They blocked the intersection, without leaving any lanes open, and when I got there I kept trying to negotiate with them to open up a lane, but they didn't trust us, or anyone else. They were sure that if they gave an inch and started moving their trucks, then the cops would take advantage of the movement to block the intersection completely.

Quebec had experienced the most brutal restrictions in all of Canada, including a curfew. The Rideau/Sussex crew were affiliated with a group called Les Farfadaas that had sprung up to push back against the restrictions. They had good reason to be upset and resentful. I spent a lot of time during the three weeks in Ottawa trying to build trust with those guys. They didn't have enough food, so I made sure they got some. They didn't have a food tent, so I had someone find one for them. They needed money at one point, so we made sure to get them a few hundred bucks from the cash donations that we were collecting on the ground in Ottawa.

I already mentioned the power struggle that had started with Taking Back Our Freedoms. They tried to commandeer our meetings and take over the convoy leadership, until we asked them to back off. They showed up with large bags of their swag for sale, too. I recall I found it very odd when they ended up suddenly in the room next to mine, five floors up from where they had been originally. Concerned with fundraising and the uncertainty of GoFundMe, they had also been trying to get me to set up a GiveSendGo with them.

Taking Back Our Freedoms also tried to convince me that I needed an assistant to keep up with my emails and phone messages. They were quite frustrated that they had been trying to reach me and I wasn't getting back to their texts or emails. They offered to provide me with one, who I guess would have been working for them. I said no thanks to all of it. I realized they were right about me needing an assistant, though, so I called my sister Dannette and she flew out right away to help me.

There was also Canada Unity, which was a group led by James Bauder that had joined the convoy, which had issued a bizarre "memorandum of understanding" (MOU) that talked about overthrowing the government, acting like they spoke for the whole convoy, which they did not.

James had helped with some of the route planning. The problem was that he was telling anyone who would listen that he was the main man behind the Freedom Convoy, and any journalist who wanted to make us look bad was eager to believe it. Justin Ling, who calls himself an "independent journalist" but is really just a stenographer of talking points for Trudeau and the other Liberals, was calling James the "creator of the convoy." And then Ling would publish on Twitter all kinds of Qanon-style conspiracy theories[149] that James had posted on social media that questioned who was behind 9/11, with Jeffrey Epstein and China connected in there somehow.

The thing about these populist movements is they attract all kinds, and I knew ours did. They were only making it harder for us to stay focused on our mission and easier for our enemies to paint us as lunatics. It was right around then that the CBC claimed that there were concerns about "Russian actors" behind the protest.[150] They later had to admit that there was no evidence of that.

---

149 https://twitter.com/justin_ling/status/1490803689094852612?lang=en

150 https://torontosun.com/news/national/cbc-issues-clarification-over-claim-kremlin-behind-truckers-protest

There was another lady who had been helping us from the East Coast who turned out to be a bit of a wild card and was giving interviews to the media who was also making claims about overthrowing the government, which is when I finally realized we needed to appoint some official spokespeople. So I tapped Benjamin Dichter, who I had met during my Yellow Vest days, because he was involved at the same time with protests against M-103, the Trudeau government's anti-Islamophobia censorship plan. Ben knows about politics, I felt that he was really articulate and intelligent, and he's great with the media. So I asked him to help me with my Twitter page, and to be our official spokesperson, which he agreed to do.

Canada Unity had some good guys, but the big problem was when James came out with this MOU, the media completely jumped all over it as proof that we were a bunch of insurrectionists who wanted to topple the government. It was the perfect way for them to wrongly tie us into what happened on January 6, 2021 at the U.S. Capitol. At The Globe and Mail, one of their more idiotic columnists wrote[151]: "The more we learned about the intentions of the group behind the convoy – Canada Unity – the stranger and more disturbing the picture became. For instance, we now know the group is set to arrive in Ottawa with a manifesto of sorts, a 'memorandum of understanding' it hopes the Governor-General of Canada, Mary Simon, will sign."

One former government official wrote a column[152] headlined "The MOU says everything you need to know about the truckers protest." Trudeau's national security advisor, Jody Thomas, said there was "no doubt" protesters wanted to overthrow the government.[153] This was all because of Canada Unity's MOU.

151 https://www.theglobeandmail.com/opinion/article-trucker-convoy-has-evolved-into-something-far-more-dangerous/

152 https://www.hilltimes.com/2022/02/02/the-mou-says-everything-you-need-to-know-about-the-truckers-protest/341596

153 https://www.cbc.ca/news/politics/jody-thomas-overthrow-federal-government-1.6379881

I've never even read that MOU. We eventually got someone from the Canada Unity group to go on social media[154] and say they were retracting it because they had realized that it wasn't the way to go with things. The truth is that Canada Unity and its "Operation Bearhug," which before the convoy was planning its own slow-rolls and mask-free mobbings, attached itself to the Freedom Convoy because we shared concerns about vaccine mandates and other restrictions. But James didn't create the Freedom Convoy, and he wasn't leading it, and his claims that Brigitte and Chris joined his plan are total bull. I can tell you for a fact that it was the other way around, and he was never a central part of the planning. And James has even been public[155] about the fact that he didn't like that he wasn't in control of the fundraising, and he spread stories that we had been "co-opted."

Pat King was an even bigger problem than James was. We actually tried to have him sent home on several occasions. I had started following Pat's videos on social media during the United We Roll convoy, which both he and James had been part of, because Pat had the best footage. I was aware of him mostly by reputation, which wasn't usually good. I eventually stopped following Pat's social media videos, because I thought he was a loudmouth with a huge ego who makes a lot of noise but not a lot of sense. He clearly loves to hear himself talk. I think he really does believe in freedom, and wants to see Canada made free, but Pat King's first priority always seemed to be Pat King.

Pat drove around in a Winnebago, with his mom in it, but he had his own group of truckers following him, and like James, he had brought them into the convoy. He was supposed to have done some organizing, too. But it turned out that some of the stuff he was

---

154 https://www.saltwire.com/atlantic-canada/news/were-not-lawyers-ottawa-protest-organizer-says-mou-not-meant-to-endorse-toppling-the-canadian-government-100691492/

155 https://www.thestar.com/news/canada/2022/03/26/three-key-freedom-convoy-organizers-pull-back-the-curtain-on-the-hopes-tension-and-infighting-that-marked-their-protest.html

supposed to be in charge of, he never did. I remember Cindy Parker having to scramble to find a bunch of hotel rooms in Sault Ste. Marie because Pat had been in charge of booking them but never did it.

As we were crossing from Manitoba into Ontario, Pat had posted one of his blowhard online video rants saying that "Trudeau is going to catch a bullet… [the] only way this ends is with bullets." Ben Dichter had messaged me and said this guy has got to go. We had spent so much time and effort making it clear that this was a peaceful protest, and here was Pat King talking about bullets for the prime minister! Chris and I confronted Pat in Winnipeg and he became upset, trying to explain that it was a mistake, that people misunderstood his video. The call was made to let him stay, because he had done some organizing and he had a following and he had a bunch of trucks that were part of his group. The road captains didn't want to start losing trucks from the convoy if Pat left and took his followers with him.

I don't even know how many trucks Pat had behind him, and I don't even know how many of them would have left if Pat told them to, or who would have followed him if he left. Some felt that a few of his online followers are questionable characters and I think that some people just didn't want to stir up trouble with them.

When we arrived in Sudbury for a quick stop I remember Pat coming over to Chris's truck, Big Red. He started telling me that he couldn't go to Ottawa after all because he was getting death threats, I guess from the fanatical Trudeau supporters freaking out over his stupid talk about bullets and shooting. Now, I should tell you that all of us organizers would get our share of death threats before this whole thing was through. But I was hoping this could be an opportunity to convince Pat to stay away from Ottawa. He was very controversial and after the video about bullets was circulated, I was mainly concerned for the optics of the movement overall. It only takes one bad egg.

Pat was complaining about how unfair it was that he couldn't be in Ottawa because he organized the whole thing, which I immediately corrected him about, and told him to check his massive ego. "This is not about you, this was a whole group of us, and you're going to destroy it," I told him. "If you care about this movement at all, you will not go into Ottawa."

That night, we parked our truck in Arnprior outside Ottawa and stayed in hotels in the city, waiting for the convoy to roll in the next day. I woke up to read on my phone that Pat was already up and had parked his Winnebago in Ottawa's Confederation Park.

We ended up wasting too much time trying to control the damage from loose cannons like Pat and many others, but we had no power to stop them. We were a grassroots protest, not a centrally run group. We were not in charge of anyone. Although I heard a lot of rumors about Pat while we were in Ottawa, about him waking people up out at the camps in the middle of the night, about him waking truckers up and telling them to blast their horns, I had never personally seen any of it. In fact, I only saw Pat over the three weeks we were in Ottawa maybe a handful of times. If we had a conflict, we discussed it and reached a resolution and then moved on.

We didn't have our first official press conference to talk about our demands[156] until almost a week after we got to Ottawa. That was after Keith Wilson, the lawyer that had been provided by the Justice Centre for Constitutional Freedoms, came to town and started helping us focus on our mission. It was at the Marriott hotel on February 3, and Keith introduced me, calling me the "spark that lit this fire and the leader of this organization," which wasn't accurate. But after that I was basically put in charge of holding official press conferences. Tom Marazzo, a former army captain who had come to Ottawa to help out, told me he thought I was good at speaking with the press and that I needed to do them all from now on.

I guess I found a talent I didn't know I had before. I think my experience playing in a band and being on stage was really helpful. But

156 https://winnipeg.ctvnews.ca/leaders-of-freedom-convoy-to-hold-news-conference-in-ottawa-1.5766468

I mostly feel like it was guided by God. When I would be walking into a press conference, or getting up to speak to the crowd on Parliament Hill — times that I should have felt extremely nervous and shaky and full of anxiety — I would just have this overwhelming sense of peace and calm come over me. There are still lots of times when we get up on stage with the band and I still get nervous and it takes me a few songs to kind of settle in. But when you're doing a speech, you don't have a few songs to settle in. So I would say a prayer before I went out to talk to the press, and I knew it was God, not me, that was providing me with the strength I needed.

Sometimes we would have multiple press conferences a day. We would often handpick the media we'd allow in. There were some reporters, like CTV's Glen McGregor, who were openly hostile and disruptive, and we didn't want them in there. Ben put in superhuman efforts as our media co-ordinator, but there were thousands of people there and any media outlet or politician could still pick some random bad apple and claim they represented our group. We couldn't control everyone. Take Back Our Freedoms was holding press conferences. Pat King was holding press conferences. There was only so much we could do to keep our messaging disciplined or controlled.

There were also Antifa activists mixing in the crowd and posing as truckers, while also putting nails under truck tires and spray painting graffiti. Trudeau had his official photographer creeping around, and he was the one that snapped a photo of a Confederate Flag on the back of someone's truck, and immediately began circulating it to the Liberal-friendly media.

That kind of divisive message was not what we were about and 99.9 per cent of the people there knew it. A few days later, there was another gentleman walking around in the crowd with a balaclava covering his face and a Confederate flag. The fact that he was covering his face made it pretty obvious this was a false flag operation by Antifa or someone else. And our crowd very politely asked him to leave and pushed him out of the crowd. They weren't even rude about it. They just basically said, "You're not really welcome here." They did the same to another guy who showed up out of nowhere with a Nazi flag. No one seemed to know who these people were. We just knew they weren't with us.

Then the CBC did its on-camera interview with Conservative MP Michael Cooper, in which he specifically said there may be a "small number of unsavoury characters" skulking around, but the overwhelming number of people were just there to send a message about vaccine mandates. Of course the CBC cameraman did the interview with a guy standing in the background holding an upside-down Canadian flag with a small swastika drawn on it. It was abundantly plain to anyone who saw it that the guy was trying to make a clumsy point and comparing the Liberal government to Nazis, and wasn't actually supporting Nazism. Obviously it's laughable that people who came to Ottawa to protest authoritarian government persecution would support Nazis. But everyone hostile to the convoy, including the CBC, jumped all over it anyway[157], claiming it proved we were Nazis.

The attempts to paint us as racist, violent and noxious were just what I had expected. And it was giving Trudeau just what he needed, letting him stand up in the House of Commons and accuse the Conservatives — a Jewish Conservative lesbian named Melissa Lantsman[158], no less — of "standing with people who wave swastikas." On February 1, the Liberals arranged to push four motions through the House designed to paint us as extremists[159], condemning people at the convoy supposedly being antisemitic, Islamophobic, homophobic and transphobic.

It was all complete bull. In the three weeks at the protest, I saw no antisemitism, Islamophobia, homophobia or transphobia. I saw Jews and Muslims and gays and straights and people from all over the

---

157 https://www.cbc.ca/news/canada/edmonton/edmonton-area-mp-under-fire-for-photo-of-him-near-flag-bearing-nazi-symbol-1.6333266

158 https://torontosun.com/opinion/columnists/lilley-trudeau-linking-lantsman-to-swastikas-is-disgusting

159 https://www.ctvnews.ca/politics/feds-dismiss-suggestion-they-should-step-in-as-trucker-convoy-protests-continue-1.5763207

country calling for Canada to join together and put an end to division, anger and persecution. I know that's what really scared Justin Trudeau. This really was the voice of all of Canada speaking. And he couldn't allow the public to know it.

Trudeau was able to secure his cynical victory, with his unanimous motions which he immediately celebrated on Twitter: "Today in the House, Members of Parliament unanimously condemned the antisemitism, Islamophobia, anti-Black racism, homophobia, and transphobia that we've seen on display in Ottawa over the past number of days," he tweeted.[160] The Conservatives under their then-leader Erin O'Toole, to their shame, allowed him to get away with it and probably helped Trudeau lay the groundwork for what he was planning to do to us.

That was the first major betrayal against us.

It wouldn't be the last.

---

160 https://twitter.com/justintrudeau/status/1488660359422648320?lang=en

CHAPTER 6:

BEWARE THE BOUNCY CASTLE

It still amazes me how we well-organized we were — at least when we weren't being completely disorganized.

Here we were, a ragtag group of truckers and civilians, who had come together from all different parts of Canada in just a couple of weeks to drive out to Ottawa with no idea of what we were going to do when we got there. And we were putting so much effort into monitoring and trying to flush out infiltrators and keeping the crackpots from trying to take over the whole thing.

But there were a lot of things we did amazingly well under the circumstances. We had incorporated Freedom Corporation so we could keep everything professional, and had elected a board of directors. We even had a full-on command centre at the Swiss Hotel, about a block east of Parliament Hill. Chris Garrah, Danny Bulford and Thomas O'Connor had set it up for us. The lady who owned the Swiss Hotel was just the sweetest person and she was so grateful to have us there. The lockdowns and travel restrictions had nearly killed her business. She was literally weeks away from closing down and declaring bankruptcy. Our arrival brought her some much-needed income.

When I walked into that command centre on the day we arrived on January 29, it just blew my mind. It looked like NASA Ground

Control. There were computers and monitors everywhere. People were scanning social media feeds in real time. Others were sitting on their laptops with their earbuds in, doing Zoom calls, or typing away.

It was then that I think it really sunk in for me for the first time. I just thought, "Holy crap, this is really happening!" We had a logo and were putting out press releases on letterhead! We had a media team, a social media team, a finance team, a security team, a safety team, a fuel team, a stage team, road captains, block captains, accountants, doctors, nurses, paramedics, firefighters, former law enforcement personnel, truck drivers, federal government employees, mechanics, and politicians. People from all walks of life rolled up their sleeves.

Danny Bulford and Thomas O'Connor were two other examples of some kind of higher intervention. They were exactly the people we needed, and amazingly, just when we needed them, they showed up and asked if they could help.

Danny was an RCMP officer for 15 years and one of the most genuine, high-integrity and honest people that I've ever met. He had worked in every province and territory in Canada and had actually worked on the detail assigned to protect Justin Trudeau. But, like so many great police officers, he had to leave the force in December over the vaccine mandate.

That also meant he had a lot of knowledge and experience and would be invaluable in deciphering whether incoming information was credible or not. With his level-headedness and a calm demeanor he helped us a lot in keeping tensions low because we were able to tell the truckers about what the police were up to, instead of leaving their imaginations to run wild with paranoia and fear.

Danny was also in charge of the security and had a whole force of volunteers, a lot of them firefighters from all over the country who had also lost their jobs due to the mandates and had come to Ottawa to help us. They all must have been sent by some greater power. We had just the people we needed to run a proper security operation, and I have no doubt they were a big part of helping keep trouble away.

We set up patrols at night to help keep the truckers safe from Antifa vandals and troublemakers and to make sure everyone was keeping to a code of conduct that we had put together for the protesters to ensure everything stayed peaceful and safe.

Thomas is a paramedic from Arnprior, just outside Ottawa, who was also against the mandates. He was just the guy we needed to head up a team of medics, just in case anyone got sick or needed medical attention. He worked as a medic for the City of Ottawa and so he knew the emergency routes well and the ins and outs of the EMS system, which was incredibly helpful in order for us to decrease our impacts on the emergency routes as much as possible. His role gradually evolved into becoming an incident commander. He is intelligent, honest, compassionate and we all looked up to him. He even started a GiveSendGo for me after I was arrested in July 2022, because I had lost my job and had no money coming in while I was locked up. He's just a wonderful individual.

Janet Seto and Chris Garrah on the Ground Zero committee were in charge of arranging showers and shuttles to and from the outposts and getting places for people to stay, if they needed it. They also arranged for a big crane stage to be delivered. It was already mostly set up the time the trucks got in to town, except for the sound system, which the City of Ottawa said we couldn't have without a permit. Eventually we got a sound system from the New Blue Party, a political party headed up by Jim Karahalios, who had been setting up its own rally near Parliament Hill in support of the truckers, so that was another blessing.

That stage hosted a rotating roster of speeches and concerts. As I mentioned before, we didn't always have control over who ended up on stage, either. Jim Karahalios, Maxime Bernier, and Derek Sloan all found their way up, even though we were trying to keep things non-partisan. I went up there a few times, myself, to give some speeches, as did Chris Barber and Brigitte Belton and other organizers.

Down in front of the stage someone put a big empty water jug for people to donate cash that we could use to help keep the truckers in fuel and food. That money would then go back to the Swiss Hotel, which is where the financial operation was headquartered, and it would be counted and put into envelopes of a few hundred bucks each. Road captains and other organizers would take the envelopes out to the encampments and pass them around to the truckers. I didn't get involved, because I preferred not to be handling all that cash, but it proved to be the best way to get money quickly to the truckers who urgently needed it without getting tangled up in the red tape of the finance committee.

The road captains were also still tasked with keeping in close contact with the police once we had set up in Ottawa. They were in constant touch with the Ottawa Police Service (OPS), the Ontario Provincial Police (OPP) and the RCMP. Tom Marazzo, a former army captain who had a firm grasp of battlefield logistics, was in charge of mapping out emergency routes and truck movements.

On the way in, Chris Garrah had been working closely with OPS officer Isabelle Cyril who was just terrific: She was actually telling us what routes the trucks should follow coming into the city, the specific streets they could park on and where we could set up staging areas. On the first Saturday, a convoy came in from Windsor managed to park on Wellington Street near Parliament Hill, and the other trucks wanted to get just as close as that. We really weren't expecting that. We thought we would be parking offsite, but apparently the police just waved these guys in to start parking right in front of the Parliament buildings. That was the first really obvious sign that they just weren't ready for hundreds of truckers rolling into town.

But the police seemed to want this to go as smoothly and safely as we did. After about the first week and a half, officers would start coming to the Swiss Hotel to meet with us in person, so we could brief each other about what we knew and how to keep everything safe and sound.

The one thing we didn't have from the start, though, was lawyers. We should have realized earlier that we were really going to need some. I have to thank Brian Peckford for waking us up to that in the first couple of days.

You might recall Mr. Peckford as the former premier of Newfoundland, from 1979 to 1989. He literally negotiated the Charter of Rights and Freedoms, along with the other premiers, with then-prime minister Pierre Elliot Trudeau in 1981. He's the only surviving drafter and signatory to the 1982 Constitution. And he had been calling out the mandates and other restrictions as violations of our constitutional rights throughout the pandemic. He had launched a challenge under the Charter against Justin Trudeau's travel mandates, and he was working with Keith Wilson, a lawyer out of Edmonton, through the Justice Centre for Constitutional Freedoms (JCCF).

Mr. Peckford had come to Ottawa to support us. So had Dr. Francis Christian, a prominent Saskatchewan surgeon defended by the JCCF after being punished for speaking out about the dangers of mRNA vaccines specifically to teenagers and children. They got us onto a Zoom call with the organization, including JCCF president John Carpay, and Keith was on the call. We decided he was going to fly out right away to be with us in Ottawa and provide us with legal help. We were able to charter a plane that could make stops along the way to pick up some other lawyers, some of whom weren't vaccinated and couldn't fly commercial. They were also nice enough to pick up my husband, Dwayne, so that he could join us. He had been laid off during the Omicron lockdowns, and so he had time on his hands. And we missed each other.

The Democracy Fund, a new civil liberties charity, had sent lawyers to help truckers facing parking fines and things like that: Ottawa bylaw officers were constantly moving through the protest zone making easy work of their ticket quotas. But Keith was going to be the one working with me and Chris and the other organizers to make sure we didn't get into legal trouble — or to help us get out of it if we did.

Keith, who turned out to be brilliant, had brought Eva Chipiuk from his firm, who is not only gorgeous, and a damn pistol, but an amazing lawyer, too. They set up shop at the Arc Hotel on Slater Street, which was closer to the protest zone. We already had an operations room at the Arc that was handling immediate trucker needs like fuel and food, while the Swiss Hotel was where we worked on the more strategic stuff. Once the lawyers got to Ottawa, there was never a decision made without discussing it first with the legal team.

Already people were trying to pin all kinds of illegal and criminal stuff on us. There was a story about "convoy protesters" supposedly bothering the homeless at Ottawa's Shepherds of Good Hope shelter and demanding free meals from shelter staff the day after we arrived. It's not like we didn't have food, so I don't know what that was about. I highly doubt it was actual convoy participants. A January 30 news report said the "altercation lasted for hours,"[161] yet they were never identified, so we'll never know.

And everyone knows by now about the apartment building hoax. Two people were caught on video trying to set a fire in an apartment building on Lisgar Street, a kilometre south of Parliament Hill. An anti-Freedom Convoy activist named Matias Munoz[162] started tweeting on February 6 that two guys had tried to set fire to his apartment building lobby the night before and had said they were from the Freedom Convoy. The apartment residents, Munoz claimed, had annoyed protesters: "After a night of blaring horns and fireworks until 4 am, some residents had yelled & pleaded with protesters outside to stop," Munoz tweeted.

The whole story stunk to high heaven. Here was one of Munoz's tweets: "As the fire was being lit, a tenant walked by and nervously asked who they were. One admitted being part of the convoy protests.

161 https://ottawacitizen.com/news/local-news/convoy-protesters-make-for-a-really-tough-day-at-shepherds-of-good-hope-shelter-ceo

162 https://dailyhive.com/vancouver/ottawa-police-arson-investigation-freedom-convoy

The tenant quickly got into the elevator and arsonists continued to ignite the package." So the tenant just went up to their apartment as two guys were supposedly trying to burn the building down? Right. Munoz claimed the front doors had also been taped shut, but a "good Samaritan" later walked by on the street out front, saw the flames, and put out the fire. And CTV's Glen McGregor showed up at the building even before the police were called, which seems very fishy to me.

The arson attempt might have been real, I don't know, but Ottawa police knew the night it happened that there was absolutely no link to the convoy. A lot of reporters ran with Munoz's version, anyway. The day after Munoz was spreading fake news, NDP Leader Jagmeet Singh[163] stood in the House of Commons and said the protesters did it, and said it was an example of how "violence is commonplace" among the truckers. Ottawa's then-mayor, Jim Watson, blamed us for it[164], too, saying it "clearly demonstrates the malicious intent" of the truckers. Public Safety Minister Marco Mendicino kept repeating the lie a week later[165], when he used it as justification for invoking Emergencies Act.

Two people were arrested over the incident.[166] Neither of them had anything to do with the convoy, except that maybe they were trying to frame us.

There were also claims in the media that we had "desecrated" the Terry Fox memorial sculpture on Sparks Street the day we arrived. I mean, I guess if you call putting a Canadian flag on a statue a "desecration" then that says something about you. But as soon as those claims were made, a bunch of truckers went down there and took

163 https://nationalpost.com/opinion/rex-murphy-will-anyone-apologize-for-falsely-accusing-truckers-of-attempted-arson-in-ottawa

164 https://tnc.news/2022/02/07/no-evidence-truckers-involved-with-arson-but-mayor-blames-convoy-anyway/

165 https://twitter.com/truenorthcentre/status/1519320726947434496

166 https://torontosun.com/news/provincial/ottawa-police-have-charged-a-second-man-with-arson-after-fire-in-downtown-apartment

flowers and stood there with a sign that said, "we love you, Terry," and they guarded it.

In fact, anytime some loon or infiltrator or outsider would try to pull something like that to make us look bad, the truckers always responded immediately. There was some lady who was dancing on the National War Memorial and Tomb of the Unknown Soldier, and had urinated on it. I suppose she was drunk. I never saw any evidence that she had anything to do with the protest. But we got blamed, and the government fenced it off.

We had a lot of truckers who are veterans, and I guess they were not about to stand for this memorial being fenced off, so they went down and completely dismantled the fence, making sure to stack up the fencing nice and tidy, and stood guard there. They had a padre come and do daily memorial services there, complete with a bagpipe playing Amazing Grace. And it wasn't just truckers who would come, but veterans came from around Ottawa in their berets, many in wheelchairs.

I had the privilege of attending services there. I went to go and shake hands with these veterans, and just hug them and thank them for their service. And they were crying and hugging me and saying, "no, thank you," which to me was just ludicrous, compared to what they had sacrificed. But they put me in their front line, right in the centre, for the duration of their service. It was such an honour. I was completely emotional about it, and I still am right now as I'm writing about it. The veterans were very important to us from the start because they're the ones that had defended freedoms on the battlefield.

Our guys got blamed a lot for public urination. That was a problem, especially at the beginning. But it wasn't supposed to be that way. The Ground Zero team had been arranging for port-a-potties to be delivered to the main protest area in time for when the trucks were arriving, and the city had originally agreed to let them in. We had a protest permit, and we knew we had a constitutionally protected right to demonstrate, of course. But the Charter doesn't guarantee the right to portable toilets, and so we needed the city's sign-off.

But the Ottawa officials reneged on their agreement and wouldn't give us the permits we needed to get the port-a-potties in. We kept pressing them to let us get some toilets down there. Everyone was getting so frustrated by the city's game-playing that eventually Randy Hillier, who was an independent Ontario MPP at the time, sent Thomas O'Connor a faked-up permit and told him to give it to the port-a-potty suppliers as proof we had permission. Of course, Thomas was completely against it, and told Randy that the last thing he was going to do was risk going to jail for some port-a-potties.

The city was clearly trying to mess with us to try and prevent us from digging in, which is what led to the public urination problem. We did our best to avoid it. And we did eventually get some port-a-potties at one point, but only after some time into our stay, and I don't know if there were enough. So we had to rely on restrooms at local businesses around the area, and a lot of local residents would walk around and kindly offer to open their homes to people who needed a lavatory. Those of us with hotel rooms would offer to let people borrow our bathrooms and showers.

The local shops and restaurants in the area were for the most part just great. I mean, they were doing a booming business. There were a couple of Tim Hortons coffee shops in the area, and truckers are frequent customers of Tim Hortons any time of year. I don't think those shops have seen that much action in years, if ever, especially since Trudeau made all the federal workers stay home over the last two years, which badly hurt the businesses around Parliament Hill.

Our guys would be grabbing mops and brooms and they would be inside the coffee shops cleaning the floors from the snow they had tracked in, and cleaning up the bathrooms. I can't imagine the shopkeepers remembered government workers doing anything like that. So don't believe anyone claiming we were bad for business in the area. Sure, there were some stores that closed down, but we didn't make them do it. That was their choice.

The entire Rideau Centre mall closed for three weeks. Ottawa city councillor Mathieu Fleury would later tell[167] the inquiry into the Emergencies Act that it was because of "microagressions." Whatever those are, that's a heck of a reason to leave millions of dollars of business on the table. I understand there were some people going without masks. But I actually kept hearing from businesses about how respectful the truckers were being to the staff. Even Jim Watson, the Ottawa mayor at the time, would later admit[168] at the Emergencies Act inquiry that stories his officials and hostile media were circulating about truckers supposedly ripping off people's masks were entirely based on hearsay and gossip.

I even noticed that stores that had closed at the start were reopening after the first few days, after they saw that it was safe — and profitable — to do so.

Still, some of them were punished for it. The Iconic Cafe on Slater Street, which was owned by this wonderful Polish family, were cruelly evicted[169] after the convoy was over. Apparently they were told they were in breach of their lease because they weren't demanding to see vaccine passports or enforcing mask rules on the truckers. That's so petty and vindictive. They were so friendly and helpful to us. I know they were trying to raise money on GiveSendGo to help them start again, so please consider helping them out if you can.

I actually noticed a theme that people whose roots were in formerly communist countries, or currently undemocratic ones, were often among the most understanding of or even grateful for what we were

167 https://nationalpost.com/news/politics/downtown-ottawa-councillors-say-they-felt-abandoned-by-local-police-during-convoy-protest

168 https://nationalpost.com/opinion/rupa-subramanya-justin-trudeaus-case-against-the-freedom-convoy-falls-on-its-face

169 https://www.facebook.com/Iconiccafeottawa/

doing. These were people who, unlike a lot of Canadians, understood the real evils of government tyranny, because of what communists and dictatorships had done to their countries. People whose families came from Eastern Europe, especially Poland and Ukraine, and even from Iran and South America, were usually the most emotionally affected by the protest. I can't even imagine the fear and the persecution that these people had to endure.

They would come up to me and hug me and start crying because they had a genuine and well-earned fear that the terrible things they had left behind were happening again. One older fellow came to my hotel one night during the first few days because he was worried for our safety. He was sure troops were coming to round us all up. He had survived imprisonment and torture under the Soviets and was traumatized. His wife was with him, and she was shaking with fear.

Honestly, I had so many people come up to me and just start crying. A lot of them were people who had come out for the protest, but a large number of them were Ottawa locals. We had so much support in that city, even though the loudest voices were the angry ones like the mayor and the anti-convoy activists. Locals were so kind. They brought us money, blankets, coffee and food. They let us use their homes if we needed a restroom. A lot of them were federal civil servants who had been badly affected by the lockdowns and mandates.

The word I kept hearing was "hope." I have the tears of thousands of Canadians on my shoulder, who every day told me that we were bringing them hope.

All the attention I was getting was actually causing a lot of tension with Brigitte and it's where things between us really started to go badly. Chris, Brigitte and me would be down on Parliament Hill, but people would be coming up to me to talk to me and hug me and get their photos taken with me. I had been doing all the Facebook Lives from the road, and the press conferences, so I guess I had become the most recognizable face for them. But I could feel that Brigitte's resentment was growing towards me.

I really worked to avoid it. When people would come up to me, I'd always grab Brigitte and bring her over to introduce them to her, and say she was one of the founders of the convoy. I would chat with her throughout the protest and try to explain to her that I didn't ask for this, that I certainly never got involved seeking this kind of attention. And I always thought that those talks ended well. But it didn't seem to be enough and she would eventually turn completely against me.

I'll note that the whole time I was with the convoy protest, I never got COVID as far as I know. That's interesting when you think about how many thousands of people I was with over the course of a month. How about that? I'm not vaccinated. And I was breaking all the rules the government said I needed to follow. And I never got COVID.

Chris and I did get sick when we got to Ottawa, because we were both so exhausted and dehydrated and we'd been running on so much adrenalin and so little sleep. I remember one of the doctors that was in Ottawa supporting us, one of the ones who was punished for daring to speak the truth about vaccine risks, he took us up to our room, and he had ivermectin and all these vitamins, and he was putting some meds in Ziploc bags and writing prescriptions on the baggies with a Sharpie pen. It was surreal. I remember thinking, wow, so this is where we're at — doctors practising underground medicine because the state is trying to stop them from dispensing prescriptions that will help people. I never thought I would see that in my country, but there it was.

It was clear to me early on that the government's plan all along was to try and provoke us so they could justify coming in and crushing us, because everything we were doing was exposing how their whole narrative was a complete fraud. I can imagine how frustrated they were that we were just being peaceful and exercising our right to protest. The OPP especially kept telling us how happy they were with our level of co-operation and how we were working with them and keeping emergency lanes open.

The worst thing that they could accuse us of was the trucker horns that were blasting. But even for me it got to be a little too much after a few days. But there was nothing we could do: the truckers were free to honk if they wanted to, and we couldn't control them. One of the Ottawa residents who is now part of that class-action suit against us, Zexi Li, went to court using a noise bylaw complaint and got the judge to issue an injunction ordering the honking to stop. To be honest, it came as a relief.

Now, the road captains could take the order to the truckers and tell them they needed to stop. And — what do you know? — they did. They obeyed the court order. We kept peacefully obeying the law, which I'm sure must have been driving Trudeau nuts.

He was trying to tell people how scary we were, but the atmosphere was like a giant, happy street party.

There were barbecues and sing-a-longs and dancing. How terrifying.

There were street hockey games. How horrifying.

There was a hot tub. And a jumbotron.

I forgot to bring one of my guitars with me. On one of my Facebook Live broadcasts on the drive up with Chris, I mentioned that I wish I would've brought one, but I didn't know how much room we were going to have and what things were going to be like when we got to Ottawa.

When I arrived, a gentleman by the name of Al had sent a beautiful little Gretsch acoustic guitar to the hotel and it was there waiting for me. Dwayne had brought his guitar out, too. Most of the lawyers were musicians, it happened, so the weekend after the lawyers and Dwayne got there, we had a jam session. Chad Eros, the accountant, played, too. We all used it as a chance to decompress after our first week. The seven days we had been there had felt so intense and chaotic.

A few days before, Neil Young had demanded[170] Spotify pull his music from the streaming service because he was mad at Joe Rogan for hosting vaccine skeptics on his Spotify podcast. So we made a point of playing some of Neil Young tunes. Keep On Rockin' in the Free World was a favourite, of course. We also played some Johnny Cash: Folsom Prison Blues.

I call that Gretsch guitar my freedom guitar. I have it hanging on my wall at home and it's got signatures from the road captains and some of the doctors who were in Ottawa who had been punished for speaking out about vaccine injuries. And of course, Mr. Peckford.

Despite all the chaos that had been going on that first week, the truckers had been their own best PR. The photographs that were travelling across Canada and around the globe showed everyone just how friendly and peaceful we were being. The truckers just handled it brilliantly. The entire world could see with their own eyes that this was a perfectly reasonable and respectful act of civil disobedience. The model of peaceful protest. I'm sure that was something else that was driving Trudeau nuts.

The truckers had set up a bouncy castle for children, for heaven's sake. At that point, even the Liberal-friendly media was struggling to make us seem menacing.

But behind the scenes, Trudeau's people were working as hard as they could to do just that. Evidence revealed by the Emergencies Act inquiry[171] showed that Trudeau's national security advisor, Jody Thomas, suggested to police that they should look at the kids that were there with some protesters and Thomas played up the idea that the kids were being mistreated. "Looking at it from a child welfare perspective, exposure to nose [noise], and diesel fuel can be a major

---

170 https://www.hollywoodreporter.com/business/digital/spotify-neil-young-joe-rogan-1235081916/

171 https://www.rebelnews.com/public_order_commission_documents_reveal_the_threat_to_take_truckers_kids_came_from_trudeau_s_inner_circle

issue," transcripts show Thomas saying on February 6. "Can action be taken …?" Thomas wanted to know were "enforcement officials addressing the children in the trucks?"

Sure enough, two days later, Ottawa police went public[172] to the media with so-called concerns about children in trucks and said they wanted to discuss enforcement with the Children's Aid Society of Ontario.

What a terrible thing to threaten. And what great way to transform a peaceful protest into an uproar. But Trudeau was looking for violence, and he would clearly take advantage of people's kids to do it if he had to.

At the inquiry into Trudeau's use of the Emergencies Act, the commission saw evidence of text messages[173] that showed one of his advisors was talking about Mendicino, the public safety minister, trying to set up media interviews where he would compare us to the Trump supporters who rioted on Capitol Hill on January 6, 2021. They were going to have him talk to the media about "some of the more extreme elements" of our group, as a way to fabricate the story that we were dangerous.

About a week into the protest, the Ottawa police really tried instigating things when they raided our camp and stole our supplies. We had people doing field procurement, getting gas, food, tents, generators — whatever it was, if we needed it, they could almost always figure out how to get it. John Skubik was our finder of all things: If I needed a food tent to help out the Les Farfadaas guys at Rideau and Sussex, he found it. If I needed breakfast food for some truckers, he found it. If we needed generators or fuel, he got it. He ended up being a jack of all trades.

---

172 https://www.rebelnews.com/public_order_commission_documents_reveal_the_threat_to_take_truckers_kids_came_from_trudeau_s_inner_circle

173 https://www.ctvnews.ca/politics/texts-show-feds-planning-communications-strategy-before-freedom-convoy-arrival-1.6132630

The staging area for supplies was in the parking lot of the RCGT Park, a baseball stadium on Coventry Road, about five kilometres east across the river, where there was a big parking lot. That was also where a lot of truckers were parked.

Locals would just drive up to the RCGT stadium with their pickups and have four or five jerry cans of fuel they wanted to donate. We would also have bulker trucks come in to deliver gas. They couldn't come right into the protest zone, so we would fill up jerry cans there, and load them into pickup trucks that would deliver them to smaller distribution hubs we had around the protest sites. From there, volunteers would put two or three gas cans on a sled or a wagon and take them out to the individual trucks.

On the night of February 6[174], dozens of Ottawa police officers raided the baseball diamond. They had snipers on the rooftops and they stole our supplies. They seized a fuel truck. They stole hot dogs, for heaven's sake. But within two hours after the raid, the logistics guys had already replaced double the fuel that had been taken.

The unbelievable thing was that it was the Ottawa police themselves that had arranged for the truckers to use the baseball diamond. As I mentioned before, Chris Garrah of the Ground Zero team had been working on advance planning in co-operation with OPS officer Isabelle Cyril. He kept the text conversation from January 26 where she told him "Hey Chris! We've secured the RCGT [baseball stadium] — 302 Coventry Rd for the convoy coming from the east. You can start working on a shuttle for them."

After they raided the stadium, the police issued warnings that anyone planning to help the protesters get more food and fuel would be in trouble. Anyone seen with a jerry can would be arrested. This was in minus-28-degree weather, so the truckers needed gas to keep their heaters going or they'd freeze.

174 https://www.cbc.ca/news/canada/ottawa/ottawa-coventry-stadium-fuel-camp-police-1.6342023

And so what did all the brilliant, peaceful protesters do? They all started carrying around jerry cans filled with water, or just empty cans, with nothing at all, so the police couldn't tell who was bringing gas and who was just walking around with an empty can. Locals joined in, too. There were jerry cans everywhere. They even held a jerry can fashion show on the stage one night. It was the perfect, peaceful way to show the cops they couldn't stop us. "It does provide a layer of logistical complexity to us," Ottawa's then-deputy police chief admitted[175], after hundreds of jerry cans began showing up everywhere. After that, the cops mostly gave up on trying to stop us from getting fuel.

But it was clear at that point that things were starting to change. The cops that were there at the start, who were being cheerful and helpful, they all started to disappear. And new police officers who didn't look familiar were being rotated in. And they seemed a lot less friendly.

On February 8, a couple days after the raid on the baseball diamond, Ottawa police roughed up a 78-year-old great grandfather[176] who had been driving past the protest and had honked his horn in support. His name was Gerry Charlebois. They pulled him out of his minivan and twisted his arm, pushed him onto the ground and shoved him against his van. I stayed in touch with his family for a few weeks after that to make sure he was doing OK. He was pretty badly bruised up and of course was mentally quite traumatized.

The Ottawa Police Service is probably one of the most disorganized, chaotic organizations I've ever encountered. We could tell that one hand never knew what the other one was doing. It would eventually become clear to the world, through testimonies at the inquiry into Trudeau's use of the Emergencies Act, that the OPS was in total shambles. The rank and file seemed to have almost no respect for the chief at the time,

---

175 https://nationalpost.com/news/canada/ottawa-protesters-employ-gas-can-subterfuge-to-frustrate-police

176 https://torontosun.com/news/provincial/warmington-arrested-78-year-old-great-grandfather-meant-no-harm-by-honking

Peter Sloly, who was hired in Toronto and seen as an outsider, and there was ongoing infighting within the force.[177] Meanwhile, Sloly was promising things[178] to Ottawa residents about cracking down on the convoy that he couldn't deliver on.

Before we even got to Ottawa, Sloly had assured everyone we were only coming for a couple of days and then we'd leave, even though we had told everyone we were planning to stay for much longer. The OPS had no idea what they were doing. Sloly would eventually resign. But as far as I know, the only OPS officer who faced any discipline over the convoy was a constable named Kristina Nelson who donated $55 to our cause and was charged with "discreditable conduct."[179] All for the crime of offering a few dollars of support to help with the care and feeding of some fellow Canadians.

Those of us at ground level could see how poorly run the OPS was run, and we were even hearing it from other police forces that were trying to assist the Ottawa police. After the raid on the baseball diamond, an Ontario Provincial Police officer actually called us to apologize for the ineptitude of the Ottawa police, telling us that the Ottawa cops hadn't notified any of the other forces about the raid, which other forces saw as a provocation.

I actually have a recording of that call from the officer, who we only knew as Officer Pierre. We had put him on speakerphone so all of the road captains could hear it, too. "I personally want to apologize… We discovered we were not being told the truth [by the Ottawa Police Services], or actually, we discovered we were not being updated and being consulted with what was going on," Officer Pierre said. "The upper management of Ottawa police they have their own reasons, that I'm not privy to, being with the Ontario Provincial Police, but I just

177 https://nationalpost.com/news/politics/ottawa-police-inquiry

178 https://nationalpost.com/news/politics/ottawa-police-made-enforcement-promises-during-freedom-convoy-it-could-never-keep-acting-chief

179 https://ottawacitizen.com/news/local-news/ottawa-police-officer-pleads-guilty-to-discreditable-conduct-for-donating-to-freedom-convoy

wanted to touch base, because we [the convoy organizers and OPP] have been working together and trying to solve a few issues... and I think we were making some good progress."

"They [Ottawa police] were not even aware of their own police service putting out this Facebook page and tweet about deciding to start arresting people that are bringing in the gas or supplies to Parliament Hill, downtown or to anywhere there's a protest," Officer Pierre said. "So I just wanted to let you know that we were not aware of that."

He even said there were Ottawa police members that he was hearing from that were completely disappointed in the raid. And he said OPP was going to "step back" from helping the Ottawa police for now because the city force was such a disaster.

Two days before we arrived in Ottawa, Justin Trudeau said he'd been exposed to COVID and needed to isolate. The day we got there, he fled the capital to an "undisclosed location." He didn't show his face for a week, and when he did, it was from the seclusion of the prime minister's cottage on Harrington Lake. He had 50 RCMP officers guarding him there.[180] He was hiding from his fellow Canadians, far away behind a wall of Mounties. He was hiding from the same peace-loving truckers that he once compared to brave war heroes.

But that didn't stop him from tweeting about us. Trudeau was determined to fight against us, but he would do it on his terms: from the seclusion of an RCMP-guarded cottage, pretending to be in COVID isolation, tapping out tweets on his iPhone:

"[O]ver the past few days, Canadians have been shocked — and, frankly, disgusted — by the behaviour displayed by some people protesting in our nation's capital," he wrote in a series of tweets on January 31.[181] "I want to be very clear: We're not intimidated by those who hurl abuse at small business workers and steal food from the homeless. We won't give in to those who fly racist flags. And we won't

---

180 https://paulwells.substack.com/p/at-ottawa-city-hall-a-convoy-of-solitudes

181 https://twitter.com/JustinTrudeau/status/1488225322025820162

cave to those who engage in vandalism, or dishonour the memory of our veterans. There is no place in Canada for this behaviour. So, to those responsible: It needs to stop. And to those who joined the convoy but are uncomfortable with the symbols of hatred and division on display: Be courageous and speak out. Do not stand for, or with, intolerance and hate."

In this show of toughness and bravado from his heavily guarded Harrington Lake hideout, Trudeau had managed something impressive: he got every single fact wrong. The supposed abuse, the stolen food, the racist flags, vandalism, and dishonouring of our veterans, the "intolerance and hate" — all had proven to be bogus accusations against us. Every last one.

But Trudeau was looking to escalate. He needed to. Using the Emergencies Act would require a justification that we were a threat to national security. And he had badly wanted to use it.

We'd find out at the Emergencies Act inquiry that the RCMP and the OPP were getting signals from the federal government[182] in just the first few days of the protest that the Trudeau government wanted to invoke the act. On February 5, just six days after we got to Ottawa, RCMP Commissioner Brenda Lucki texted her counterpart at the Ontario Provincial Police to say that either her force or his could be asked to lead the response "if they go to the Emergency Measures Act" (a previous name of the act, before it was renamed).

Lucki even said she was trying to tell the Trudeau government to slow down, but it's "not easy when they see cranes, structures, horses, bouncing castles in downtown Ottawa."

Trudeau, still laying low in his hidey hole, was evidently thinking of using the Emergencies Act because he had heard there were bouncy castles and horses in downtown Ottawa. They call Ottawa "the city

182 https://nationalpost.com/news/politics/texts-discussing-invoking-emergencies-act

that fun forgot,"[183] so he must have figured that people having simple fun in the nation's capital called for emergency action.

Actually, Trudeau had been talking about deploying the Emergencies Act even before that. Even before the convoy was a gleam in Brigitte Belton and Chris Barber's eyes.

Trudeau had been signalling he was pondering using the Emergencies Act as early as March 2020 — almost immediately after the pandemic first started.

It was March 24, 2020.[184] Ironically, it was in one of the same speeches where he stopped to give special thanks to truck drivers for "keeping the country running." He was performing one of his very grave-sounding speeches from in front of Rideau Cottage. That's the government-owned residence where he spent months taking cover from the House of Commons, announcing hundreds of billions of dollars in spending and ordering strict new pandemic crackdowns without consulting the people's representatives in Parliament.

In 2020, during what we were told was a historic global crisis, the Trudeau government, with the unprincipled co-operation of the opposition parties, arranged for the House to sit just 64 days from the day the World Health Organization declared COVID a pandemic, barely half the average number of sitting days since 1975, and a good number of those few days were virtual, or cut short.[185] And that's when Trudeau wasn't proroguing Parliament and shutting it down altogether[186], as he did the following year to stop parliamentary investigations into the WE Charity scandal where he awarded a

183 https://www.cbc.ca/player/play/2440045244

184 https://pm.gc.ca/en/news/speeches/2020/03/24/prime-ministers-remarks-updating-canadians-measures-respond-covid-19

185 https://nationalpost.com/opinion/np-view-emergencies-act-just-the-latest-example-of-trudeaus-contempt-for-parliament

186 https://en.wikipedia.org/wiki/WE_Charity_scandal

$900-million sole-source contract to friends of his, who had also hired Trudeau family members for lucrative gigs.

In that speech in March 2020, Trudeau had come out of his Rideau Cottage seclusion to announce more "emergency measures." But then he dropped this in:

"The federal Emergencies Act is a last resort, but as I keep saying, all options are on the table. If people do not comply with expert advice and government guidelines, we will have to take additional steps."

Pardon me? This was just two weeks after the WHO had declared the pandemic. Chief Public Health Officer Theresa Tam was still telling Canadians they didn't have to worry about wearing masks. It was just a week[187] after the Trudeau government had finally caved to pressure from the public to start limiting international flights, including from China, after lecturing Canadians that even carefully screening travellers from COVID hotspots like Wuhan was not just pointless, but racist.[188]

And the prime minister was already talking about using the Emergencies Act, which lets the government enact emergency laws without having to get parliamentary approval, "if people do not comply with expert advice"? The Emergencies Act is the successor the War Measures Act. It's never been used before and was intended only to be used when something threatened the security of Canada and — this is the important part — no other existing laws are sufficient to deal with the threat. We were a couple of weeks into a pandemic, Trudeau's so-called experts had no idea what they were doing, and he was already talking about going nuclear. There is something severely disturbing about that.

This wasn't just a trial balloon, either. A couple of weeks after that, Trudeau sent a letter to the premiers of the provinces and territories to

187 https://www.ctvnews.ca/health/coronavirus/canada-shutting-the-border-to-most-non-citizens-due-to-covid-19-pm-trudeau-1.4854503

188 https://nationalpost.com/news/canada/first-reading-pandemic-border-closures-suddenly-arent-racist-anymore

test their support for invoking the Emergencies Act. Consultation with the premiers is required by the act, although the prime minister can still invoke it, even if they don't all approve. The trouble for Trudeau was that every last premier told him they opposed the idea, and so he backed off for a while.

Trudeau was obviously desperate for an opportunity to use the Emergencies Act, but he kept striking out. And so it's no surprise that in just the first few days after the convoy arrived in Ottawa that his government was already chomping at the bit to invoke the act, as RCMP Commissioner Lucki's texts showed in the Emergencies Act inquiry. This time, it was apparently the RCMP and the OPP — the police themselves — who were trying to get Trudeau to chill the hell out and not use what legal scholars have called "the stiffest government emergency powers of any emergency law in Canada" to deal with a peaceful protest on Parliament Hill.

The Liberals have always been jealous of the political dramas in the United States. They wanted their own "January 6th uprising" like the incident at Capitol Hill in 2021. Their text messages proved it. But for that, they needed us to be dangerous, they wanted to feel like they were defending democracy against us. It must have enraged Trudeau that we weren't giving him what he wanted. We were peaceful. We were pro-democracy. We were pro-constitution. We were pro-Charter rights. We had proven we weren't just a fringe.

Trudeau had been signalling he wanted to use the Emergencies Act so he could play-act as a defender of Canadian democracy, but there was no threat. That's why even police were stunned when he actually did it.

Because the police, local authorities, the truckers and even the federal government all knew that before Trudeau invoked the Emergencies Act, we had already struck a deal with the City of Ottawa to start clearing the trucks out.

CHAPTER 7:

HOLD THE LINE

It was obvious that Jim Watson was freaking out within the first couple of days after we arrived in Ottawa.

In early 2022, Watson was the mayor of Ottawa, the capital city of Canada, a city which gets all kinds of protests all the time. So you would think he would understand that protests come with the territory. Even protests that he may not personally agree with, from people who come from parts of Canada that he would prefer not to associate with.

I get it that there had never really been a protest that went on for weeks before, and I would understand it if he was starting to lose it at the end. But it seemed like the guy was out of his mind with rage almost right from the start.

On January 31, just two days after we got there, Watson started doing the rounds on TV political shows on CBC[189] and CTV[190] denouncing us. He said any political support for the convoy was "unacceptable" and "despicable." He called the protesters "disgraceful" and "boorish," and blamed us for wreaking havoc and violence. He said we had been "smashing" windows of ambulances and city vehicles. He accused us of "harassing" and "threatening" local retail workers,

---

189 https://www.youtube.com/watch?v=EPRREYb6zFo

190 https://www.youtube.com/watch?v=9FLdHh92PlA

and "stealing." He called us antisemites and racists. Not a word of it was true.

Two days after that, on February 2, Watson's then-chief of police, Peter Sloly, said[191] Watson's municipal government had already been talking about calling in the military to clear us out. The chief had reservations about that because soldiers are not trained to deal with local police issues or civil protests.

When Watson invoked a city-wide "state of emergency" on February 6, just a few hours before Ottawa police raided the baseball diamond and stole our hot dogs, he called it "the most serious emergency our city has ever faced." I don't know about that. I still remember the time an Islamist terrorist attacked the Parliament Hill area, killing Corporal Nathan Cirillo, who was guarding the National War Memorial, and shooting up the House of Commons. We were participating in a peaceful protest. There were speeches and sing-a-longs. There were conga lines. I think Watson had completely lost perspective.

The next day, Watson wrote[192] to the federal and Ontario governments demanding that they send in 1,800 OPP and RCMP officers to clear out what he called a "siege" of Ottawa. "The demonstration has turned into an aggressive and hateful occupation of our neighbourhoods," he wrote in the letter, which was also signed by the chair of the city police board.

"Given the scope and scale of the armada of large trucks that are now occupying our downtown core, we are writing to you today to ask that you work to help the city secure 1,800 officers to quell the insurrection that the Ottawa Police Service is not able to contain," he added. "We must do everything in our power to take back the streets

---

191 https://nationalpost.com/news/canada/police-chief-considering-all-options-including-military-help-to-end-ottawa-trucker-protest

192 https://www.saltwire.com/atlantic-canada/news/ottawa-mayor-calls-for-feds-to-provide-1800-more-police-to-clear-protesters-100690157/

of Ottawa, and our parliamentary precinct, from the criminal activity and hooliganism that has transpired over the last nine days."

An "aggressive and hateful occupation"? An "insurrection"? Talk about unhinged. And this guy was calling us the lunatics?

I knew Watson had reasons to be frustrated with his police force. They clearly had no idea what they were doing. But like Trudeau, the mayor had decided right from the start that we were an unacceptable fringe minority, a bunch of unwashed hooligans from those lesser parts of Canada who should be denied our rights to peacefully protest in the nation's capital.

Brian Peckford and Keith Wilson, the lawyer who the Justice Centre for Constitutional Freedoms had flown out from Edmonton to advise us, began talking about how we needed to help find a way to take some of the pressure off Watson. He wasn't coping. We were constantly working to keep things running smoothly with the police, even after the stadium raid. But Watson was really starting to piss the truckers off with his fake accusations and insults.

Another one of those perfectly timed miracles was right about when Dean French showed up. Dean was a big operator in Ontario politics, and had previously worked as the chief of staff for Ontario Premier Doug Ford. He had been having conversations with Mr. Peckford, who he knew from before, and said he wanted to meet with us. Dean said he had been in touch with some official people, but he wouldn't say who, and he wanted to know if we'd be interested in negotiations. We didn't know if he was a messenger for the prime minister, or the police, or the city or the province. He was worried that tensions were rising and that there was a growing risk that something bad could happen.

It's true that things were really heating up with breakout protests happening at the border crossings. The first one had started in Coutts, Alta., at the Montana border, the day we arrived in Ottawa, January 29. Then, on February 7, a bunch of trucks showed up at the Ambassador Bridge between Windsor, Ont. and Detroit, and blocked that, too.

The border blockades were as much as a surprise to me as to anyone. We weren't connected to them. We didn't advise them. We didn't organize them.

It wasn't until nearly a week after the Ambassador Bridge blockade that we decided we should finally address the border protests: I wrote up a statement on February 13 with help from Ben Dichter and Joanie Pelchat, a Quebec road captain who also was our official translator, who would put it out in French. It read:

"I wish we could take the credit for the blockades, but we cannot. This movement has captured the hearts of Canadians and the entire world. We are aware that Canadians nation-wide are feeling inspired by the truckers' resolve here in Ottawa and are starting their own convoy demonstrations as a means to show support for ending mandates. We wish them well and are so heartened to see how organically this movement is spreading. We of course encourage all demonstrators across the country to be peaceful just like we have been and continue to be here in Ottawa. We are all keeping an eye out on the protests and blockades happening nation-wide and insofar as we are concerned, it only strengthens our demonstrators' resolve. It is within everyone's right to speak out and stand-up for freedom, and that is what our convoy is about. We thank everyone in all parts of our country for their support — we couldn't have accomplished so much without you."

I remember I was a little uncomfortable with the wording. We supported the protests at the border, but again, we didn't want to support illegal activity. It was hard to get both things across, so we did our best to try to express our mutual support while still making it clear we were only interested in peaceful protest.

The border blockade was what finally set Ford off. He had been mostly trying to ignore the protest in Ottawa and hoping it would just go away. That seems to be his default management style for most things. He talks tough sometimes, but he seems to always take the easiest way out. Ontario ended up with some of the worst pandemic restrictions in the western world because Ford always went along with whatever the most maniacal public health militants demanded.

When another convoy inspired by us announced it was coming to Toronto on February 5 to show its support, Ford started calling our protest "unacceptable" and an "illegal occupation."[193] But when the border blockades started, that's when Ford told his attorney general to go after us, and they tried to seize our GiveSendGo money. On February 11, Ford declared a provincial state of emergency. But like Trudeau, he still wouldn't meet with us. So we found out Dean French wasn't working with Ford. Ford apparently wasn't interested in talking to us, either.

Of course, Dean also knew the mayor of Ottawa from when he was working at the premier's office, and it turned out that's who Dean was representing. After talking with Mr. Peckford and Keith Wilson, Dean reached out to Watson to see if he would be willing to start negotiating with us. We had actually been talking to the city even before Dean came to town.

On February 8, the same day Dean arrived, Tom Marazzo, with Keith Wilson and Eva Chipiuk, had gone to a secret meeting with the Ottawa city manager. We all knew that things were getting to be on a knife's edge. And we were hearing through our intelligence networks that the police were preparing a raid on the protest camps. The earlier police raid on the baseball stadium had only inflamed things and broken down trust, without moving us an inch. No one wanted another confrontation.

But the city and the cops wanted to relocate trucks that had been camped out east blocking the intersection of Rideau Street and Sussex Drive, which was a few blocks north of the main protest zone. That was the group of Quebec truckers, Les Farfadaas, who we had difficulties with the start because they refused to leave any emergency lanes open.

193 https://www.cp24.com/news/doug-ford-makes-statement-ahead-of-toronto-convoy-protest-calls-situation-in-ottawa-unacceptable-1.5768560

They had been willing to open a lane up temporarily on an as-needed basis, but that just wasn't practical. The organizers all agreed we needed to keep emergency lanes open, so we were willing to help the city make it happen, if the police wouldn't raid us. We knew it would help lower the temperature on all sides. But it wasn't a sure thing. Until then, we had never been able to get these guys to budge.

The police had only made matters worse by boxing these guys in with a bunch of concrete barricades. The Quebec truckers were sure that if they gave an inch, the police would start backfilling in the space with more barriers, pushing them out.

Keith and I went to talk to them. It took a lot of convincing. They were sure it was a trap. The Ottawa police had double-crossed us before, so there wasn't a lot of trust left. There were three trucks we were going to move from the intersection and we were instead going to let them park in prime spots on Wellington Street. We eventually convinced them that this would be a win for us all, because it would stop the police raid that we had heard was coming and it would take pressure off the city and the mayor and put it back on the prime minister, where it belonged.

On February 9, we had both the city and the Quebec truckers on board with the plan. I sent out a message to the road captains on Signal, which was the app we used as our main communications channel with the group:

"We need you on standby tomorrow morning for a very strategic and ESSENTIAL move about Rideau Corner. This will get the city off our backs and put pressure on the Feds....This is a MUST happen. If the raid doesn't happen tonight it's because of this move ... This must happen. It's the most important move we can make. These guys need to understand this. It's a deal worked out by Eva to prevent the raid tonight."

A few of the captains immediately responded with skepticism. They knew how difficult these Quebec guys had been. And Chris Barber said he thought people liked that the Quebecers were blocking the route for

Trudeau to get back to his house. "We have fucked that corner up for PM getting home. Good luck getting the French to move," he wrote.

The next day, on February 10, the police brought a crane truck in to move the concrete barricades they had used to box these guys in. We had informed all of the road captains, but not all the protesters had been told this would be happening. And because of the tensions that had been rising with the police and the city, a lot of people were on edge. When they saw the police bringing in this crane, word started to spread through the protest camps that the police were starting to tow the trucks away.

There were about seven police officers there, and they had hooked up one of the barricades to the crane, and all of a sudden one big guy just sits right down on it. So I went over to him. I'm just a little person — I'm five feet tall and insignificant — and here's this big fella who just plunked himself right there. So I went over to this guy and I said, "You know, this is a good thing. We have a deal with the city. We're going to move these trucks up to Wellington. This has all been agreed upon. I appreciate what you're doing, but it's not warranted." So he said, "Oh, OK, great." And he hops off the barricade and leaves.

But when I turned around, I saw that a massive crowd of people had appeared. One guy started shovelling snow onto the barricades to stop the police from being able to hook them up to the crane. I tried talking him down, telling him that we had made this deal, but he was very agitated and talking about vaccines and masks. And so I'm running around in this crowd trying to tell all these people that this is OK, and this has all been planned, and we were working with the city, and going to move these trucks up to the Hill. But it wasn't working. And then they started chanting "Freedom." And some of them started singing O Canada.

And suddenly, for the first time since I left Medicine Hat, I was scared. Everything around me felt very intense. It felt like it could go very badly. I could see how these people could turn in a split second against these police officers if they felt they were being played. I became very concerned for how this was going to go, and I had a moment of panic where I thought, "We've got to get this under control. We don't want anybody to get hurt." I've seen these things on the news before. I've seen peaceful crowds turn into riots when they're provoked. That's when it became a reality for me, how easily that whole attitude could have changed from one of love and peace to "these police officers are trying to screw us over."

Keith and I talked to the police and we told them we didn't think the plan was going to work. And thankfully the police agreed, and called it off, and left. But we were back to not having made any progress in our negotiations.

The mayor was under the gun and running out of options and the premier was very upset over the blockade at the Ambassador Bridge, which is the most important border crossing for commercial goods for both Canada and the U.S. On February 10, Ford declared a provincial state of emergency.

Dean French flew into Ottawa on February 8. With things starting to come to a head, it was just in time. He threw a secret pizza party on the 24th floor of the Ottawa Westin for us. It was me, the lawyers, and some of the road captains. And we spent the time just getting to know each other and building up trust with each other. He didn't indicate that evening who he had spoken with at the city. We would later find out it was Jim Watson.

Even though Watson clearly despised us, it was obviously in his best interests to negotiate a deal with us. We knew there were a lot of residents hounding him and his staff because they were mad that we were there. And we had incentive to negotiate, too. We still didn't have an exit strategy, and we needed to start moving toward de-escalation and eventually to an end game. We had been away from home for weeks. We were tired. People wanted to go home. All we wanted was someone in power to meet with us and talk to us and hear us out. I was starting to sense that protesters were starting to get irritated as politicians and the Liberal-friendly media continued to goad us. I was seeing more flags that said "Fuck Trudeau." I saw a group of women shouting "shame, shame" at a CBC reporter. I didn't like how things were shifting to more negativity.

Our beef wasn't really with the City of Ottawa, anyway. If the mayor was willing to dignify us with a discussion, we thought maybe provincial and federal leaders would also start seeing it was worth talking to us. For all his attacks against us, we were grateful that the mayor was at least now finally willing to treat us like human beings.

We let Dean know that we were willing to start moving trucks out of residential areas around Ottawa, and relocate them to some outposts around the city and farms outside the city limits. We wanted the city to drop its local mandates, too, but we knew that we needed to show some good faith on our side first. We had never really planned to have trucks on residential streets to begin with, so we were open to the idea of just keeping a core unit of trucks in the most immediate downtown core.

But we wanted to make sure we could still hold protests downtown. We'd leave the trucks at the farms and the outposts, but if we were giving them up, we needed to be able to shuttle people in to the downtown. So one thing we were firm about was that we needed some buses to help us do that. It took a couple of more meetings between us and Dean, and Dean and the city, and the lawyers and some city staff. Then, on Sunday, February 13, 2022, we announced the deal. We agreed to remove all trucks from the residential districts and the baseball stadium and we promised that no other trucks would come to replace them.

Of course, it was easier said than done. Jim Watson got to speak for the city. We weren't like that. We were a grassroots movement. I couldn't speak for all the truckers. I had to take the deal back to the road captains and we had to go around getting buy-in from the truckers themselves. If they didn't want to move, we weren't going to be able to make them do it. And after what had just happened at Rideau and Sussex, there was no guarantee it was going to go smoothly.

On February 12, the day police moved in on the border blockade on the Ambassador Bridge, Chris Barber, Tom Marazzo, Eva Chipiuk and organizers Ryan Olson and Joe Janzen met at city hall with then Ottawa city manager Steve Kanellakos, as well as Kim Ayotte, the city's general manager of emergency services and Robert Drummond, the Ottawa police superintendent. Kim Ayotte had shown on the maps where they were willing to let us keep some of our trucks. The city reps also talked about how they needed the baseball stadium cleared because, even though it was owned by the city, it had been leased out. Everyone agreed that we needed to change things up after two weeks of protesting.

It was going to be tricky. I guess Watson didn't want to be seen as weak by negotiating with us, because that would piss off the Ottawa lefties. We had a lot of suspicious people on our side, too. There were some people badmouthing me, saying I was negotiating with the city behind the truckers' backs, that I was selling out. But when I went out and talked to the truckers about what we were planning, most of them liked the idea.

We co-ordinated a heavily orchestrated plan. There would be an exchange of letters between the mayor and us. The first came from the mayor. It was addressed directly to me. It read:

Ms. Lich,

The protests in our city, and the occupation of certain residential districts by a large number of trucks, is now entering its third week. My overarching concern is for the safety and security of our residents, business owners and workers in the downtown core, who are innocent collateral damage of this unprecedented national and international demonstration.

Our residents are exhausted and on edge, and our small businesses impacted by your blockades are teetering on the brink of permanent closure.

I don't believe these harmful effects on our community and its residents were the intended consequences of your protest.

That's why I am writing to ask that you remove your convoy and its trucks from all of our residential neighbourhoods and that you restrict your presence to a limited perimeter from Wellington Street where it meets Elgin Street and to the Sir John A. Macdonald Parkway.

I ask that you immediately seek the support of the truckers to follow this path of de-escalation. I would offer to meet with you to discuss your protesters' concerns, as long as you respect the following conditions:

1. Remove all trucks from the residential districts south of Wellington Street, and from all other residential areas including the market, the Ottawa Baseball Stadium on Coventry, etc.;

2. Agree to not backfill the residential areas currently occupied with trucks, other vehicles and/or demonstrators; and

3. Agree to not displace the truck convoy, vehicles and/or demonstrators to other residential areas in the City of Ottawa.

I want to see clear evidence that the truck convoy will be departing the residential areas before noon on Monday, February 14. I am asking you to collaborate with local authorities to protect the adjacent communities as the convoy exits.

As the departure of the over 400 trucks from residential areas is a significant logistical undertaking that will probably take 24 to 72 hours, we ask that protesters stop asking more demonstrators to come to Ottawa this weekend, in order to assist the truck convoy to depart the residential districts in a manner that ensures the safety and security of residents.

I look forward to your protest movement meaningfully delivering on these steps as a show of goodwill towards our community. Once there is clear evidence that you have delivered on these commitments, I am prepared to meet with you in a timely fashion.

I hope we can make progress to alleviate the extreme and undue burden this protest, and the occupation of our residential districts in the core and elsewhere, have had on the residents and businesses of downtown Ottawa. A copy of this letter is also being provided to your legal counsel.

Sincerely, Jim Watson, Mayor, City of Ottawa.

We issued a response the same day, written from me:

Dear Jim Watson

Thank you for your letter.

The truckers here in Ottawa have always been about peaceful protest. Many of the citizens and businesses in Ottawa have been cheering us on but we are also disturbing others. That was never our intent.

The Freedom Convoy Board agree with your request to reduce pressure on the residents and businesses in the City of Ottawa.

We have made a plan to consolidate our protest efforts around Parliament Hill. We will be working hard over the next 24 hours to get buy in from the truckers. We hope to start repositioning our trucks on Monday.

As stated in your letter, we look forward to working with authorities to ensure the safe movement of our trucks to their new locations.

Please reach out should you have any questions. We look forward to meeting with you to discuss the issues raised by the truckers.

Kind regards, The Freedom Convoy 2022, Tamara Lich, President."

That day we sent a memo out to be distributed to the truckers to let them know we had been working on a deal:

CONFIDENTIAL

Date: February 12, 2022

From: Tamara Lich

To: Ottawa Freedom Convoy Truckers

Subject: FREEDOM MANIFEST

We began our freedom convoy with a clear destination. Restoring freedom for our families, our neighbors, and our country.

We rolled into Ottawa 2 weeks ago taking a stand for our future.

We have given hope and power to freedom-loving Canadians and beyond. People from around the world are now standing behind us and want us to win.

We have to stay in Ottawa for the long-haul to reach our destination. Just like we do every day with our routing logistics, we have to plan for the road ahead.

Route Map:

We all know that the Prime Minister keeps wanting us to make mistakes so that he can use force to get us out of Ottawa and extinguish our freedom movement.

We have parked our trucks throughout Ottawa but the pressure needs to be on our political leaders at Parliament Hill to act to restore our freedoms.

We have always been about peaceful protest. Many of the citizens and businesses in Ottawa have been cheering us on but we are also disturbing others.

We need to reposition our trucks so we don't give the Prime Minister the excuse he desperately wants to use force and seize our trucks.

The truckers on the Freedom Convoy 2022 board plan to start repositioning our trucks forward on Monday to consolidate our protest to the streets in front of Parliament. There is also room for trucks to relocate to [the outpost on highway] 88.

We will be working with the Road Captains on the details.

It was signed by 12 organizers: Me, Chris Garrah, Ben Dichter, Chris Barber, Brigitte Belton and Joanie Pelchat, as well as captains Sean Tiessen, Miranda Gasior, Chad Eros, Joe Janzen, Dale Enns and Ryan Mihilewicz.

We finally had a deal. When the news broke, Ben Dichter was pissed. We had put his name on the letter, but he really didn't support the deal. He sent out a tweet calling it "fake news," saying there was no deal: "No deal has been struck, the federal government has not yet lifted its mandates and passports." I had given him access to my personal Twitter account, and he used my account to retweet it. I tweeted a correction later that day, confirming we had made a deal with the City of Ottawa.

The plan was to start moving the trucks on Monday, February 14.

That morning, Justin Trudeau announced he was going to invoke the Emergencies Act for the first time in its 34-year history.

The Emergencies Act wasn't even used on 9/11. Or the terrorist attack on Parliament Hill. Trudeau was using it against a protest for freedom, against people who were draping themselves in the Canadian flag. Right after we had made a deal to move the trucks. He didn't want this to end peacefully. He wanted a fight.

My husband Dwayne had flown into town on February 2, hopping a ride on the chartered plane that Keith and the other lawyers had flown in on. On the morning of February 14, Dwayne and I, and Keith and Eva were heading to the Lord Elgin Hotel to meet Brian Peckford. We were on our way to meet with the last living signatory of the Charter of Rights and Freedoms when we heard about Trudeau announcing he was going to use the nuclear option to override Canadian law and suspend democratic rights. Trudeau said he was going to hold a press conference about it later that day.

I remember we walked into the room at the Lord Elgin and Keith told Mr. Peckford about what Trudeau had just announced. Mr. Peckford's face fell. "Good Lord," he said. He grabbed the arm of a chair, and he sunk down into it in shock.

Trudeau had blown everything up.

Trudeau obviously realized he was about to lose his chance to finally use the Emergencies Act, which he'd been trying to do for two years, since the pandemic first started. Trudeau called it a "last resort." But he had spent weeks refusing to talk to us. He hadn't even bothered trying a first resort.

Mr. Peckford was aghast — and livid. He had been planning to do a press conference that day with some of the doctors who had been speaking out about vaccine risks. He cancelled that. "Tamara and I need to do a press conference. We need to do it at 3 p.m. We need to pre-empt the prime minister's own press conference. I don't want anybody else there." He cancelled the doctors. I asked if we should have some of the road captains come and stand behind us, and he said no. He said, "We have one message and one message only. We don't need any distractions. If the media starts asking you any questions, I'll answer them."

We held our emergency press conference at the Sheraton Hotel with me and Mr. Peckford.[194] We wanted to show Trudeau, and more importantly, the people of Canada who supported us, that we were not about to be intimidated and crushed by a power-mad prime minister. Our main message to our truckers, our supporters and Canadians, was going to boil down to three words:

Hold. The. Line.

I brought a prepared statement and I read it out before Mr. Peckford took questions. Here's what I said:

I am honoured to be sitting next to the last surviving founder of our Charter of Rights and Freedoms: the very document that is now being used against the people it was designed to protect.

The federal government is planning to invoke the never-before-used Emergencies Act. First of all: We are not afraid. In fact, every time the government decides to further suspend our civil liberties, our resolve strengthens and the importance of our mission becomes clearer.

We will remain peaceful, but planted, on Parliament Hill until the mandates are decisively ended. We recognize that there is a democratic process within which change occurs. We have never stepped outside of that process and nor do we intend to.

All Canadians should be surprised — no matter your political opinions — that such an extreme measure would be used against a peaceful demonstration. We have countless vulnerable people in our crowd, including children, the elderly, and the disabled, who cannot be met with force by a genuine liberal democracy. The right to peaceful protest is sacrosanct to our

---

194 https://rumble.com/vuyezi-v2-truckers-staying-even-with-emergencies-act-freedom-convoy-leader-and-cha.html

nation. If that principle is abandoned, the government will reveal itself as a true tyranny and it will lose all its credibility.

In that unfortunate situation, we have faith that politicians, police officers, and military, will listen to their conscience.

Remember: 'I'm just following orders' has always been an excuse used by those who ignore their moral intuition.

But we have faith in you, Canada, to do the right thing. Do not let this become a dark moment in our history.

I want to now address all Canadians: we love you all. Some of you might oppose our grievances. However, democratic society will always have non-trivial disagreements and righteous dissidence. There are many reasons for us opposing the mandates. Some of us have been mistreated by our government, including our many Indigenous communities who have personally experienced medical malpractice. Some of us simply want bodily autonomy and oppose the mandates on principled grounds. No matter the reasons and opinions, it is how the government responds to its citizens that determines the fate of the country. Listen to your hearts Canadians: Is the Emergencies Act the right response to our demonstrations of love and freedom?

Now, I want to address the prime minister. No matter what you do, we will hold the line. There are no threats that will frighten us. We will hold the line.

Lastly, to our truckers and friends on Parliament Hill: Do not give in to fear and threats. Your courage has already exceeded all of our expectations, and inspired an international movement. Be strong. Show kindness. Love will always defeat hate.

"HOLD THE LINE."

The media was packed into that room and Mr. Peckford handled them all. The one question that was specifically directed at me was from CTV's Glen McGregor, who had been the most hostile and obnoxious reporter throughout the convoy. He asked me something about the illegal firearms that they had reportedly found among some protesters at the Coutts border, and could I guarantee that there were no firearms in any of the trucks in Ottawa.

Everyone groaned and booed him. It was a stupid question, first of all. How would I know? If he wanted to know if the truckers had weapons, he could walk around and ask them all individually himself. Secondly, he was just using weapons as a trigger. The prime minister was about to run roughshod over Canadian law, and Glen McGregor was still trying to make us out to be the criminals.

Trudeau was telling Canadians he needed the Emergencies Act to clear the border blockades. But the Ambassador Bridge and the Coutts crossing had both been cleared before the Act took effect. It was just another lie. He wanted to use it to crush us.

After the press conference, we all went upstairs to a conference room at the Sheraton, and Mr. Peckford came up with his wife and sat with us for a couple of hours and told us all stories about when they were drafting the Charter of Rights and Freedoms, and stories about Pierre Elliott Trudeau, and Peter Lougheed. He even told us tales about Réne Lévesque's womanizing. It was such an honour just to be in his presence.

We all watched Justin Trudeau's press conference from there together. It was surreal. Here we were with a man who, along with Pierre Elliott Trudeau had guaranteed Canadians' rights, and we were watching the son, Justin Trudeau, steamrolling over it all. It was a very heavy moment.

Trudeau's deputy, Chrystia Freeland, announced that they were going to start coming for our bank accounts and insurance.[195] But she also kept talking about the border blockades, which the Act wasn't even needed for. "This is about following the money," she tweeted. "This is about stopping the financing of these illegal blockades. We are today serving notice: if your truck is being used in these protests, your

195 https://twitter.com/cafreeland/status/1493387961571987456

corporate accounts will be frozen. The insurance on your vehicle will be suspended."

The next day, on Tuesday, Ottawa police chief Peter Sloly resigned, and his deputy, Steve Bell was made interim chief. After the bad experiences we had with the Ottawa Police Service, I remember people telling me they thought it was awesome. They were celebrating. I told them I didn't think it was awesome at all. It meant something worse was going to come. And I was right.

Sloly has taken a lot of blame for things he apparently did wrong during the protest. But I think he's been a convenient scapegoat. I don't think his resignation was voluntary. It would come out later, in the Emergencies Act inquiry, that Trudeau was undermining him and telling everyone Sloly wasn't up to the job.

It also became clear in the Emergencies Act inquiry how little support Sloly had from his officers and the administration. The guy was under a lot of intense pressure and scrutiny and his team wasn't behind him. I'm not saying I think he did everything right. But I don't think he deserves to be the target of all the accusations and blame. I guess I have a little bit of empathy for him because I'm kind of in the same situation. When there's a witch hunt, they need to find a witch to pin things on. I never got to meet Sloly during the protest, but when I saw him at the Emergencies Act inquiry in October, I walked up to him on a break from his testimony and I thanked him for his service. He seemed to appreciate that.

Tuesday, February 15, was when we started noticing towing equipment start to show up around the perimeter of the protest zone. We heard rumours that there were buses coming in to start hauling us away and that they were setting up an intake facility at the War Museum. I knew that it was only a matter of time, and not very long, before I would be arrested.

Chris had gotten up early and went out to continue moving trucks off the residential streets. Keith got a call from some city staff and police officials to tell him our deal with the city was off.

On Wednesday, I recorded my final Facebook Live. I was exhausted. I was emotional. I didn't have a speech prepared. I spoke from my heart. Tears were spilling down my face. My voice was choked up. But I'd never felt stronger, prouder or more honoured to be a Canadian. Here's what I said:

Well, it's been quite a day. I'm not really sure where to start. I really wanted to get up on stage before everything happened here and send a message out, but I think I can do it here and it'll probably even reach more people.

This has been a crazy ride. A really crazy ride. And I think in one of my first videos I said how proud I was of all of you, so proud of you you've come together in a way that I've never seen before. I just wanted to come on again and say, first of all, thank you. Second of all to say, please keep that love in your heart. Don't give in.

You know it's been an incredible experience here and there has been a lot of joy and a lot of happiness. And so the tears that I cry aren't tears of sadness. They are tears for what has happened and what is transpiring against my fellow Canadians. It breaks my heart. It is breaking my heart, you guys.

I just want you to stay strong and I want you to continue to be unified and spread the love. I have to ask you, I've seen people rightful... well maybe not rightfully so — I can't tell you what to do — but you know, when you see the reporters in the streets, be kind and show them love. We don't have to agree with what they're doing but it upsets me when I see people upset with them... After all they've done, I know, I know, it's frustrating. But we still have to have love in our hearts. Please show respect to them.

Show respect to our police officers. A lot of these men and women, although I know it's not an excuse, are probably just trying to feed their families. I said it from the start and I'll say it again, please pray for them and forgive them for they know not what they do. At least, I have to believe that.

And I know there's a lot of anger at our government. There's a lot of rightful anger at our government. But I want you to know that Justin Trudeau has three beautiful children, so remember that we don't have to like what he does, but I'm going to ask you to pray for him, too. And I'm going to ask you when you fly a Fuck Trudeau sign, remember that he has three kids — just like me.

I pray that you all find forgiveness in your hearts and I pray that you will find love even when we don't understand it. Because there's lots of things that I don't understand. There's a pretty good chance — well, I think it's inevitable at this point — but I'll probably be going somewhere tomorrow where I'll be getting three square meals a day and that's OK. I'm OK with that. And I want you to know that I'm not afraid. I'll probably get some sleep, finally.

Just please stay peaceful and please take care of each other. I know that this too shall pass. And I'm not sure if you remember, but I posted a video few weeks ago — if feels like forever ago — about 'tomorrow' and there will be a tomorrow and we will get through this.

You have to understand that there's a lot of things at work here that need to prevent this from being a success. And the only way that this is going to succeed is if we always come from a place of love I've always said as human beings we make choices from one of two places: we make choices from love or we make choices from fear. That's it. That's the bottom line. And I pray and I hope that you will make your choices from love.

You have to know that they're trying to provoke us. I mean, you hear their language. You hear the language and the verbiage that they're using — and that is not coming from us, and I know you guys all know that. But we can only win this with love and we can only win this together. And it's time to stand together.

If you can come to Ottawa and stand with us, that would be fantastic. And if you can't, pray for us. I know you are. I just want you to know that this is my hill, and the hill of so many brave men and women. I can't tell you how amazing these people are and they're going to stay and they're going to fight for your freedom as long as they possibly can.

The road captains that I have just had the honour of spending so much time with became my family and my trusted friends and I know we're going to have summer vacations together and we're going to have Christmas together and I can't wait...

I know I'm crying but it's not tears of sadness. It's definitely not tears of fright. Like I said, I'm just so damn proud of all of you. Every single one of you. Not just in Canada, but all around the world.

Who knew? Who knew that this was going to take off in this way? So please try not to be angry. Keep love in your heart. Stay strong. Stay unified. And stay proud. Because we are so proud of you. The love we have felt in the last 19 days — well, before then, actually. I guess we left on the 24th.

Like I said, it feels like it's been a year all across this country, the likes of nothing I have ever seen before. And that was you guys. That was all you.

So, I'm going to sign off — for now, anyways, don't you worry, I'll be back. I want you to keep fighting the good fight and I want you to look out for each other and I want you to have each other's backs. I think you're all amazing... [and] all the people that are here on the ground that have worked so hard ... you're all heroes, man. All of them .

The stuff that you don't see in the videos, and the stuff that is behind the scenes, there's too many people to mention. But they are all here for you. They're here for you. So tomorrow is a new day and I'm ready. I am not afraid. And we're going to hold the line.

Thank you. I love you guys. See you soon.

I expected it wouldn't be long before they would be taking me in.

I had no idea how hard it would be to get arrested in that town.

CHAPTER 8:

'COME AND GET ME'

There were dangers around us even before we got to Ottawa. Once we got there, it seemed we were always on high alert.

We knew that the RCMP and the Canadian Security Intelligence Service would be monitoring us. We knew that any number of law enforcement and security agencies would be spying on us. When we had meetings in the hotels we had people leave their phones outside. We searched for bugs. We used encrypted messaging to communicate. We assumed our phones could be tapped.

There was one woman named Dagny Pawlak, a lovely human being and just a gorgeous little thing, who had been helping out Ben Dichter with media. I'm not even sure how she got to us. People found out somehow that she had once campaigned for Barack Obama and had been involved with the Liberal youth wing. They found a photo of her with Liberal cabinet minister Marco Mendicino. Every day people would come up to me and tell me she must be a plant or a spy.

Everybody was always accusing everyone else of being a spy and a plant. There were rumours that some undercover agents from Antifa had joined the convoy in Winnipeg. Some people even suggested I was secretly working for one of the political parties. Chad Eros suspected me and Keith of secretly working for Taking Back Our Freedoms, because Brian Peckford is part of that group and we had been working with him.

I don't think Dagny was working undercover, although I do think there were plants in the protest. I think some of them are still hanging in or around our group. We made a joke about the Dagny suspicions and nicknamed her "Deep State Dagny." But there was so much paranoia, I'm not sure everyone was convinced it was a joke.

I had been moving around to different hotel rooms. I had first stayed at the Arc Hotel, but I had to move out. The Arc had become a magnet for all these different groups that were jockeying against each other. There was also a safety aspect. I had received death threats and was told the Arc staff had received threatening calls. It was best if I changed locations.

I had relocated to the Sheraton only a block over and shortly after being there we saw cameras in the office window across the street pointing up to my room. I don't know who that was, but I was definitely not into it. So I moved to the Swiss Hotel.

After Trudeau invoked the Emergencies Act, the dangers felt much more real. It had always been difficult for us to decipher which threats we were hearing about were based in reality and which ones were wild rumours. But now that the government was resorting to war measures, it became nearly impossible. There were games of broken telephone happening everywhere, with stories changing as people passed them along. At one point, word started spreading that the police were bringing in a sound cannon — a weapon that blasts these loud noises that are like torture and that drive you crazy so you have to run away. Danny Bulford said he didn't even think one of those existed in Canada.

What we didn't know then was that the RCMP was working on the assumption that we were armed, which was totally untrue, but made things a lot more dangerous. If they were treating us as if we had weapons, they would treat the situation as much more dangerous and be much more inclined to see shooting at us as justified.

The Emergencies Act inquiry would discover that the RCMP sent a briefing note[196] to the Liberal cabinet on February 14, the day that Trudeau invoked the act. "Intelligence information also suggests that convoy protesters are beginning to weaponize themselves," it read. "Officers are constantly monitoring the shift in behaviour and will respond accordingly." The Ottawa Police Service later confirmed[197] that the only "weapons" they ever found after they started arresting people were tire irons and knives — things you might find in any truck.

But the lies kept coming. On February 16, Mendicino, the public safety minister, had made another completely hysterical and false claim[198] that protesters were committing "deadly" crimes. "Dangerous criminal activity occurring away from the TV cameras and social media posts was real and organized," he said. "We're talking about a group that is organized, agile, knowledgeable and driven by an extremist ideology where might makes right, and this is completely contrary to our democratic values." It was a total fabrication.

In fact, Superintendent Patrick Morris, commander of the Intelligence Bureau of the Ontario Provincial Police, would later testify[199] that police officers "weren't seeing much evidence" of any extremism, and that "the lack of violent crime was shocking," and he criticized politicians and members of the media for spreading those lies.

A text message that came out at the inquiry into the use of the Emergencies Act showed that RCMP Commissioner Brenda Lucki

---

196 https://www.theepochtimes.com/rcmp-falsely-claimed-freedom-convoy-protesters-were-armed-documents-show_4793855.html

197 https://www.blacklocks.ca/count-tire-irons-as-weapons/

198 https://www.theepochtimes.com/rcmp-falsely-claimed-freedom-convoy-protesters-were-armed-documents-show_4793855.html

199 https://nationalpost.com/news/politics/opp-sent-ottawa-police-intelligence-warning-freedom-convoy-would-stay-long-term

was being pressured by the Liberals[200] to write a letter endorsing the Emergencies Act, so they could justify its use. "Has Minister Blair hit you up for a letter to support the EA [Emergencies Act]?" she texted to OPP Commissioner Thomas Carrique on February 19.

The actual truth didn't matter to the federal government. The Liberals were aggressively building a phony case to justify the Emergencies Act — and for the use of violence against us.

Danny started briefing us on what we needed to know if we were arrested based on his deep experience as an RCMP officer. He told us not to resist, to just identify ourselves. Some people were saying they were going to be defiant, and if the police came to arrest them, they would do this or that. And Danny was telling them not to be stupid. If they put up a fight or caused any friction they were just going to end up in more trouble.

He said if we were co-operative, here's what would happen: They would take us to the police station, they would keep us there for maybe a few hours, or possibly overnight, and then we would have to sign some kind of guarantee and we would be released pending a hearing.

That's not what happened to me.

Some of the truckers had started leaving the downtown area after Freeland threatened their insurance and bank accounts. Some had relocated to the outposts. The threats were a real danger for a lot of truckers and trucking companies, because they can't work without insurance or banking.

I didn't even have a truck, but my bank account was frozen. My husband and I had a joint account, so he was frozen, too. I don't even know if I'll ever get a mortgage again. Chris Barber had a successful trucking business for years and he's been red-flagged at the bank and

---

200 https://www.theepochtimes.com/rcmp-commissioner-suggests-minister-blair-asked-her-to-express-support-for-emergencies-act-text-messages_4826873.html

can't get credit anymore. His son, who's also a truck driver, has been turned away, too. It's really hurt them.

Certain groups that were trying to make this all about them split town right away. I still wasn't entirely sure what to expect. I've never been through anything like this. The City of Ottawa had called a state of emergency and that really didn't affect us. It just meant that there were more police officers standing around doing nothing than there were before. Ontario had issued a provincial state of emergency, and all we saw from that was even more cops standing around doing nothing. So I honestly didn't know what to expect with this Emergencies Act. I thought, well, this could get really ugly or it could just be just another scare tactic.

We had been in Ottawa for nearly three weeks and we still hadn't put out an official statement as to what we were there to accomplish. We started working on it as soon as the lawyers, Keith and Eva, arrived that first week. It was supposed to be our exit strategy. The plan was to draft a manifesto, I would read it out on Facebook Live, and as I was reading it out live, we would email it at the same time to all the federal party leaders and all the provincial and territorial premiers.

We had gotten pretty far with it in the first week. We came up with things that we absolutely wanted to see happen, and we came up with some throwaway demands that we could use as negotiating tools, things we were willing to give up as part of a negotiated agreement. But every time we would try coming up with a plan for the right time to release it, something else would happen and it wouldn't be the right time. This went on for weeks, which was quite frustrating. Then we were going to do it on February 14th, after our deal with the City of Ottawa was official, and Trudeau pushed the Emergencies Act button.

On February 16, I finally had a final draft that we were ready for me to read out on Facebook Live and send, simultaneously, to the party leaders and premiers. Our board had approved it. Except, even that didn't go smoothly. It never did get emailed to the political leaders at the same time as I was reading it out on Facebook, which had been our plan all along. To this day, I don't even know if it was ever sent. In fact, after I finished reading it, Ben and Dagny wanted to tinker with it some more because they thought the language in it wasn't flowery enough and they wanted to soften the tone. It was ridiculous. I told them it was too late — I had just finished reading the whole thing out to the whole world. How could we change it now?

Here's what it said:

February 17, 2022

Open letter to our premiers, and to our elected and appointed officials.

End the mandates; end the vaccine passports. This is why we are here.

We began our Freedom Convoy with a clear destination: Restoring freedom for our families, our neighbours, and our country. We arrived in Ottawa 20 days ago, taking a stand for our future.

We have given hope and power to freedom-loving Canadians and beyond. People from around the world are now standing with us and want their freedoms back.

Today, February 17th, 2022, we continue to inspire millions of Canadians to resolutely demand the return of their freedoms. We have furthermore become the model — the beacon of hope — for citizens across the globe.

The government-imposed restrictions in the effort against the COVID-19 pandemic, which rescinded many of our liberties for our "protection," have been worse than useless. For instance: families have become separated; children, who require intimacy and play for their educational and social development, are suffering the consequences of inhumane isolation; small businesses, especially the service industry, can no longer survive with limited capacities; mental health issues such as drug addiction, alcohol dependency, and suicide have increased several fold.

The list of harms is too many to document here, and others will emerge with time. All we can do now is heal the damage that you have done.

The concept of "freedom" here is not only an idea; we have materially felt its loss. Otherwise, we would not be in the streets. Many of us now have nothing to lose. This is our line in the sand. This is where we hold the line.

Once we arrived in Ottawa, we experienced a truly Canadian gathering. The Sikh communities shared food with everyone. Dance parties were set up. Concerts with sea shanties were held. Children drew thank-you cards for truckers and handed roses to police officers in between playing street hockey, drinking hot chocolate, and jumping in bouncy castles.

We have heard Canadians far and wide. Here we communicate what has been conveyed to us.

The message is clear: End the mandates, end the vaccine passports. This is why we are here. We are calling on all governments in Canada to restore the rights and freedoms of Canadians and set concrete limits so governments can't easily abuse our rights and infringe on our freedoms again. The message is as follows:

1. *We call upon our governments to restore the rights and freedoms of all Canadians:*
2. *End federal, provincial and municipal vaccine passports.*
3. *End masking requirements.*
4. *End all state-of-emergency declarations pertaining to our peaceful protests.*
5. *Provide financial protection for the small businesses harmed by COVID restrictions.*
6. *Respect freedom of choice without discrimination.*

Furthermore, Canadians want assurance that our governments will not repeat the same mistakes again. We propose the following steps be taken to ensure this.

1. *Supreme Court of Canada Review of Government Actions*

   We need to know whether our rights under the Charter mean anything. We call upon the federal government to initiate a Constitutional Reference Question to the Supreme Court of

Canada about the constitutional validity of the COVID laws and restrictions.

2. *Public Inquiry of Government's Response to COVID*

   As a matter of national importance, Canadians call upon the federal government to appoint a fully independent and impartial public inquiry on the government's handling of COVID responses.

   We need to know what went wrong — what caused governments to so easily trample our rights and freedoms and cause so much harm to our people and our nation.

   For the inquiry to be effective, the following conditions must be considered:

   a. *The inquiry members are to be selected by an all-party parliamentary process;*
   b. *It must contain a thorough examination of the science, internal communications, policy responses, and the consequences;*
   c. *It must be commenced by March 20, 2022; and*
   d. *It must be made public, in the interest of transparency.*

The Freedom Convoy has achieved so much already. In fact, we have revived the Canadian identity and our culture, which openly accepts every person with love.

We all have a choice. Please join with us and Canadians who seek freedom. This can be part of your legacy. We are uniting Canadians across the country and will accept your support, even if you've previously been reluctant. This is not about the past — this is about the future. You, too, can be on the right side of history. End the mandates. End the vaccine passports.

Yours sincerely,

Freedom Convoy 2022.

Even though we held out hope that the manifesto would help open negotiations to bring a peaceful resolution to things, we knew that the danger was still there that Trudeau and the police would make drastic use of the Emergencies Act.

Joanie Pelchat, the road captain from Quebec, and a few other people were packing up over at the Sheraton. They were going to go and stay in Saskatchewan, where one of our biggest backers, Joseph Bourgault, is from. He's an enormously successful businessman and had been a huge supporter of us in Ottawa. At one point he tried to run for the Conservative leadership, but didn't qualify.

Joanie has a daughter that she was worried about, so she wanted to get out while she could. I went to the hotel to say goodbye to her. It was very emotional. We hugged, and cried. After she left the hotel, I put my hand in my pocket and realized it was full of cash. Earlier in the day, when I was down in the protest zone, Mr. Peckford had been speaking to the crowd from the stage, and people had been stuffing cash into my pockets to help us. That happened a lot. People would just come up to me and hug me and hand me cash for the truckers. For the cause. That whole time I was in Ottawa, other people had their hands in my pockets more than I did.

I pulled out a fistful of money, it was something like $400. So I ran downstairs and found Joanie packing her car up and I gave her everything I had so she could make sure she had gas and food for her daughter.

I told my family they should leave, too. Dad and my youngest sister, Rachelle, had arrived a couple of days prior with some supplies, food and to pick up Dannette and take her back to Alberta. They had planned to get a room out of the protest zone and start for home early in the morning. I told them I thought they needed to get as far away from Ottawa as they could, immediately. We were all very sad. Dannette had been with me for a couple of weeks and had worked with me closely. It was hard for them to go. I remember walking up the hotel stairs and looking back at my dad and I said "drive safe, Dad. I love you." It was the last I would see them for a long time.

I'm not your typical religious person. I'm more spiritual. I was raised Catholic, so I have a lot of Christian influence, but I believe a lot of Native spirituality: the power of the universe, energy, that sort of thing. So I kind of have my own blend of spirituality that works for me.

But that day, I went up to my room after my dad left, I opened the door and I walked over to the bed and I dropped to my knees. And I prayed.

This was the first time I had prayed on my knees like that in I don't even know how long. I asked for strength and guidance and wisdom. And for everybody to be safe. Please, I prayed, just keep everybody safe.

I could have left, too, but I also couldn't leave. I didn't think we needed to leave. No one told me to leave. Someone showed me a screenshot of some order saying we had to vacate immediately that was supposed to be from the police, but it looked fake. It had spelling errors and didn't have anyone's signature on it. I'd seen a lot of fake photos and fake documents and fake stories in the weeks since I arrived.

The next day, I went down to the service for veterans at the National War Memorial. I spent that afternoon walking around with a veteran, meeting people and talking to truckers. We walked around for about four hours. When I got back to the Swiss Hotel, it took about 15 minutes before everybody's phone started buzzing with the news.

They had arrested Chris Barber.

Chris was just walking down the street with Joe Janzen and some of the other road captains. They were down there trying to help move trucks out. Even though the deal with the city had been pulled off the table, they were still trying to help people get out of there, because people wanted to go. The police walked up to Chris and asked him to identify himself, which he did, and they escorted him to their cruiser and handcuffed him. Joe Janzen was getting the whole thing on video. Chris was laughing and said, "This is awesome." Then he said to Joe, "Call my wife."

Danny Bulford and I were at the Swiss Hotel when we heard the news. We were all in shock. Danny and I figured we would be next. And we realized we didn't want the police raiding the hotel. Danny's wife was there, and my husband was there. We didn't want them to see us being arrested. Plus my laptop, and a lot of other things they could have seized were in my room at the Swiss.

I went back to my hotel room and I hid my laptop behind a painting on the wall. And I left my phone in the room. There was nothing incriminating on either of them, but when they arrested Chris Barber, they took his phone. Later, they downloaded all of his text messages, which is how his conversations with Brad Wall came out in the media. And I thought, well, this is my stuff, and it's nobody's business what's on there but mine.

Then I put on my freedom pants.

I call them freedom pants because they're cargo pants with eight different pockets. I put a Bible into my pocket on my left ankle. I put some braided sweetgrass into the pocket on my right ankle. In my right thigh pocket I had a thank-you letter that some children had written to me and another letter from a supporter that someone had handed me down at the protest, explaining how he and his family had lost everything because of COVID and the mandates and were living in their car.

I had a small cameo of the Virgin Mary that someone had given to me in one pocket. In another I had a rose quartz crystal shaped like a heart. And I also had the Charter of Rights and Freedoms.

Those were my freedom pants. I took great satisfaction in knowing that the police who arrested me would be annoyed by having to inventory all of it.

And then Danny and I decided to go find some police officers and try and turn ourselves in.

It was about 7 p.m. It was getting dark. Snow was falling. We started walking the five or six blocks up towards Parliament Hill. Sean

Tiessen, a road captain from B.C. and John Skubic, our logistics guy, were with me. We weren't sad then. We weren't angry. We weren't upset. We were determined.

We were even joking around. I remember I said that as we were walking down the street to meet our destiny, it reminded me of Star Wars, that we were like the rebels going to face the Empire. I was Princess Leia, of course. And we were laughing about who else was Luke Skywalker and who was Chewbacca.

I had the attitude that they're not going to scare me and I wasn't going to let them intimidate me. If they wanted me, here I was. "Come and get me," I thought. "I'm not afraid of you."

We came upon a group of three girls, and they were quite happy and jovial and they gave us a hug. I told them, "Grab your phones and come with us," so they started following us. And then a few paces up, there was this beautiful young photographer, and so she took our photo, and I told her "Bring your camera and come with us." So we walked up to where the stage was, turned and took a left and went down Metcalfe Street, and there were two white Chevrolet Suburbans parked with their headlights facing Parliament. We could tell they were police vehicles.

We walked down to the SUVs and knocked on the window. When the officer rolled it down Danny said, "Excuse me, sir. I think you're looking for us. We're some of the organizers of the convoy and we understand that you're making arrests."

The officer asked for our names and then he rolled his window back up. He talked on his radio. He rolled his window back down. And then he said, "No, I don't think we're looking for you."

Danny asked him if he was sure, because they had arrested Chris Barber earlier in the day. So the officer rolled his window up again. And he got on his radio again. And he rolled his window down again. And said, "Nope, we're not looking for you."

I thanked the officer and pointed up to Parliament Hill and told him that if he decided he was looking for us, we would be up there. Then we started walking away. After a few minutes, I turned around, and I saw that the Suburbans were leaving. It all struck me as very strange.

We spent at least an hour after that mingling around on the Hill, talking to people. I was with Dagny when we came across a French-speaking couple with two young children. Their little girl was holding this little Canada flag and she was just the cutest thing. Dagny was holding a sparkly balloon and asked the little girl if she wanted it. And I asked if I could have a picture with her and her mom agreed. That was the last photo that was taken of me before I was arrested.

Danny, Sean, John and I started heading back to the Arc Hotel because that's where Sean was staying and he needed to get some stuff. We warmed up there for a few minutes and then we left and started walking towards the Swiss Hotel. It was already quite dark because they were doing a lot of construction in that area, so the lights weren't all working and the area was not well lit.

We came across a couple that met us there, walking towards us, and the woman recognized me right away and started crying and hugging me. Then, suddenly, a white Chevrolet Suburban goes flying past us. Then another. Then another. And then a fourth one came and pulled up right beside us. And I said, "This is it, here we go."

I told the woman to get her camera out. John took his phone out, too. Two police officers got out of the SUV. They asked if I was Tamara Lich and I said, "Yes, I am Tamara Lich." And the cop said he was going to place me under arrest. And I said, "OK." I remember the officer did not identify himself, which I thought was odd. I turned around and stuck my hands behind my back, and they put on the handcuffs.

As the officer walked me to his cruiser, Sean yelled out "Hold the line!" and I yelled it back to him. I also heard someone yelling at one of the officers and I asked them to stop and to be respectful.

They sat me in the back of the SUV, and one of the officers started reading me my rights. As he was doing that, I remember looking out the window, at all the buildings around me, thinking about all that had happened, and realizing that it was all over now. And then I heard the police officer say, "Are you listening to me?"

I said yes, and I repeated that he had just said, that I had the right to legal counsel, or whatever it was, to show I was listening. Then he finished and they took me down to the police station on Elgin Street.

They got me out of the truck and two female police officers came out of the building to search me right there in the parking lot. They took off my coat and emptied all my pockets. They did a full search right out there in the dark and freezing cold.

They took me inside, and took my photo and took my fingerprints, and weighed me in. Then they put me into a tiny little cell with a metal toilet, a metal sink and a cement slab for a bed. It had been snowing and wet all day. My boots were wet. My sweater was wet. I asked for a blanket. They said they didn't have one.

I was freezing. I was exhausted. The concrete was sucking what little warmth I had out of my body. So I just waited there. Danny had told us that it was very likely if we were arrested, we would sign an undertaking and be released within hours, as this was the normal procedure. I figured I would be out soon enough. That night, or the next day.

The government was going to make sure I wasn't.

CHAPTER 9:

THE DUNGEON

I don't know how they arranged to get Moiz Karimjee assigned as Crown prosecutor to my case, but I don't think it was an accident.

Karimjee is a loyal ally of Justin Trudeau and he doesn't even keep it a secret. As the True North Centre recently discovered[201], Karimjee has been donating lots of money to the Liberals for years.

Since 2013, he's donated over $17,000 to the Liberal Party of Canada, but gave just a few hundred dollars to Conservative causes. He was invited to a "donor appreciation" celebration for Liberal backers who gave more than $1,500 a year. Justin Trudeau was there. So was Trudeau's then-principal secretary Gerald Butts and his chief of staff Katie Telford.

No wonder Karimjee has made it his obsession to have me locked up. He'd see to it that I would spend 49 days in prison. And he's not done with me yet. He's tried to put me back over and over again. He'll be reading this book looking for something in it that will let him put me back in prison. And when I go to trial, sometime in late 2023, he'll be trying to get me locked up for as long as he can. He said he thinks I should face 10 years in prison.

The charge against me was mischief.

---

201 https://tnc.news/2022/07/06/lich-crown-prosecutor-liberals/

The first sign that something strange was up was when they told me they were assigning a homicide detective to my case, Det. Chris Benson. When I first got into jail, they let me call my lawyer. I called Diane Magas, a local defence lawyer who had come down several days earlier to meet with Keith and Eva and the rest of us at the Arc Hotel and told us to call her if we got arrested.

Diane told me about Det. Benson and warned me that he was a big, tough-looking cop, and told me she wasn't sure why they had put a homicide detective on the case. After the call, I asked one lady copy there and she told me she thought they assigned him "because he's very intimidating." He's about 6' 5" with a shaved head and he's really big-boned. I laughed a little because I have spent a lot of time around big guys, especially recently. They don't intimidate me.

Diane told me that if they tried to question me, I didn't have to answer anything. Det. Benson and another cop, named Pascal, took turns playing good cop, bad cop with me, but the answers they got were a lot of "No comment. No comment. No comment."

I spent the rest of that night freezing in that concrete cell. The next day they put me in handcuffs and leg shackles and sent me off in a van to the detention centre.

I had never been in prison before. But you know what? I didn't freak out. I wasn't afraid. I might have felt a little anxiety because I was uncertain about what was going to happen. But I wasn't going to let them scare me.

For close to two years they had tried to intimidate us. "You had better behave and you better do what we say," was all we heard since March 2020.

And I had spent the last few weeks putting up with people threatening me. Anti-convoy people threatening to rape me or kill me. Police threatening to arrest me. Politicians threatening to take away my house and my money.

And for all that time, they refused even to come and talk to me. To just put in the effort to listen for a while and ask us what we were upset about and what we wanted.

So I was done with their intimidation tactics. They lost their power over me. I firmly believe that this entire thing was guided by God. And if God wasn't finished with me yet, and there was more that I needed to do, and being in prison was part of it, then that's what I would need to do.

When I got to the detention centre, they made me strip down and open my mouth and show them all my other nooks and crannies. You know what I mean. They even asked me to wear a mask while I was doing it. Picture me bent over with my ass in some cops face, but I'm wearing a mask for her protection. What a reminder of the nonsensical public health "science" bullshit that we were so tired of putting up with.

They asked me if I was vaccinated, and I told them no. They offered me a vaccine, and I said no thanks. They asked me if I would take a COVID test, and I said no thanks. I have never taken a COVID test. If I don't feel sick I don't see why I should have to. And I'm not just going to take it because the state wants me to.

So they gave me some clothes, a bite to eat, a bag full of extra prison clothes and bedsheets, and they took me down to what I call the dungeon. It was solitary confinement. It was a dark cell, with high walls, with a teeny little window way up at the top. The place was covered in disgusting graffiti — swear words, drawings of naked women, all kinds of gross comments.

For the first couple of days, I just slept and slept some more. This was the first time I had gotten any real rest in weeks. And there was nothing to do in there but lay down and nap, and then wake up, and eat, and lay down and nap again.

I asked them for a book. They wouldn't give me one. They wouldn't give me a newspaper either. There was nothing to do but sleep. They would let me out to call my lawyer. They let me out to take a shower. The other 23 hours a day was spent in that dungeon, alone, with nothing to do.

My bail hearing was on February 19. They took me back upstairs, did the strip-search thing, put me back in my street clothes, shackled my legs and arms, and sent me off to the courthouse.

That was where I first encountered Moiz Karimjee.

Until I got to the courthouse, I had no idea that I was going to be cross-examined. I've never been cross-examined before. I still thought the hearing would be the lawyers standing up and saying a few things, and I would sign a piece of paper and I'd go home. So I found out five minutes before the hearing started that both Dwayne and I were going to testify and be cross-examined, because Dwayne was going to be my surety who would guarantee that I would keep to my bail conditions. We had zero preparation for any of it.

There were like a thousand people in that hearing room who had come to see me. My lawyer had to fight her way into it, it was so full. Karimjee wasn't there in person. He was doing his part online through Zoom. I was completely shocked at how aggressive he was. He started talking about how I was facing 10 years in jail. That was my first real "holy shit" moment. He was being so vicious and talking about locking me up for so long on a mischief charge. I realized then that this man was not going to rest until I was behind bars for a very long time. His questioning went on for hours.

As soon as my husband Dwayne testified, I knew I was going back to jail. Karimjee asked my husband what he did for a living and Dwayne said he was a pumpjack mechanic. Karimjee didn't know what a pumpjack was and asked him to explain it. And Dwayne said it "pulls the dragons from the ground."

Dwayne went to college to become a pastor and does a lot of Bible studies and that's how he speaks, more in analogies than anything. He was actually quoting a Corb Lund song. But Karimjee looked at him like he couldn't believe Dwayne had the audacity to speak to him like that. When Karimjee asked Dwayne something about how he felt about roads being blocked, and Dwayne shot back with a question about how Karimjee felt about people being treated badly by their government, I knew it was over.

The woman adjudicating the bail hearing was Judge Julie Bourgeois. The hearing was on a long weekend, so I had to wait in jail until Tuesday for her decision. It didn't matter, because she had decided to deny me bail.

Diane, my lawyer, had proposed that I be allowed to post a cash bond and return home to Medicine Hat under Dwayne's supervision. Bourgeois wouldn't allow it. She really tore a strip off of me. She kept referring to Ottawa as "my community." She said that about 12 times: how the protest had affected her community. I thought that was a pretty strange way for a judge who is supposed to be impartial to speak. She said I was a "high risk" to reoffend and that keeping me in jail was "necessary for the protection and safety of the public." She agreed with Karimjee that I should be treated as someone facing 10 years in prison. For mischief.

Mischief is the kind of charge they throw at teenagers who spray paint their names on playgrounds, or knock over mailboxes. It's pretty much a charge of vandalism.[202] This wasn't normally something that was considered a danger to the "protection and safety of the public."

But then we found out, surprise, surprise that Bourgeois was also a big Liberal supporter, just like Karimjee. She actually ran as a Liberal candidate in the 2011 federal election.[203] There are videos of Justin Trudeau praising her[204] when he was a Liberal MP, before he became party leader and prime minister. So my bail was being decided by a

202 https://www.oykhmancriminaldefence.com/faq/mischief-charges-canada/

203 https://ottawacitizen.com/news/accusations-of-judicial-bias-raised-during-tamara-lich-bail-review-hearing

204 https://www.youtube.com/watch?v=3HUiCJ-3cOk

former Liberal candidate who had been personally endorsed by Justin Trudeau, argued by a Crown attorney who had been invited to dinner with Trudeau to thank him for his lavish support of the Liberal party. I didn't stand a chance.

Karimjee eventually found more charges to throw at me, although he couldn't really find anything very serious to charge me with. He added obstructing police, counselling others to commit mischief and intimidation. My bail hearings were like mini-trials, but I had no opportunity to defend myself. Everything Karimjee and Bourgeois were saying about me was the opposite of what was true, but I couldn't present any evidence. They said we were blocking roads, but we had emergency lanes open and I had been trying to arrange to move the trucks anyway.

I couldn't believe Diane wasn't saying anything to counter this stuff. Maybe this wasn't the kind of forum for that. I don't know. But it was really frustrating to sit there and listen to them say this stuff about me with absolutely no recourse for me to defend myself or nobody that would stand up and say, "No, this isn't true."

I was sad that I was going back to prison instead of going home. But every day I was in there I told myself "Thy will, not my will." If this is what God needed from me, then I could do it. I had done my share of camping, so I tried to look at it that way: If I can camp in the woods, I can do jail. Of course, I had no idea how long I would be there.

I went back to solitary and I still didn't have a book. I begged them even for a Bible. I was willing to take anything. But they wouldn't give me anything. There was a TV blaring outside down the hallway, but I couldn't really see it from my cell. I remember one day they were playing the movie Jaws. I wondered, if this was some kind of torture they do on prisoners, because it was so loud. I found it wasn't meant to be torture, though. They had it blaring so prisoners can hear it and watch it from their cells.

With nothing to read or watch, I tried meditating. The cell was so gross. After a few days I decided, well, if this is going to be my room, I need to make it my sanctuary. So I took the soap and toothbrush they had given me and I started scrubbing the floor. I also scrubbed the graffiti off the walls. Most of it was just disgusting and I didn't want it in my room. But then I came across something someone had written that said: "The first 14 days of quarantine are the hardest. Brighter days are coming."

I started to choke up. And then I started crying. I thought about all the people that were thrown in jail during the pandemic. I'd never considered how hard they must have had it. They would be thrown in these cells for two weeks of isolation — at least two weeks, maybe more. There must have been so many of them. I left that bit of graffiti right where it was.

After a couple of days, they gave me a pencil and some looseleaf paper. I started using the pencil to write my own markings on a metal panel that was part of the bunk bed, keeping track of how many days I had been in there. I could see how after being in that dark room for a while you could easily lose track of the days. Then I wrote out the lyrics to O Canada, and drew a Canadian flag, and I signed my name: Tamara Lich, February 21, 2022.

After four days they moved me out of solitary confinement and took me upstairs to what they call "cell block," to share a cell with another prisoner they were quarantining. She was also named Tamara. She was in for assault, after getting into a fight with her dad and cutting him with a bottle. The two of them had been drinking and doing mushrooms together. She obviously had her demons, but I liked her. She was quiet and didn't say much. We were able to get a game of Yahtzee and some playing cards, and we just killed time together. There was room called "access," with a TV and a phone that we were allowed to visit for an hour a day. Access was a huge deal because I could use the phone there to talk to my husband and my parents, as well as my lawyers.

After a couple of days, my cellmate Tamara was allowed to move out of cell block and into the area called dorms, which is like general population, where you get more freedom. There are more common areas there, with TVs and phones, and you can move around a bit more. But there's zero privacy anywhere. They offered to let me take a COVID test if I wanted to join her, but I refused. The guard chuckled and said "Yeah, I didn't think so."

Eva had dropped by the prison before she went home to Edmonton to put some money into my canteen, which is like a fund you can draw on to buy things in prison, including long-distance phone calls, but also things like shampoo, insoles, books, cards, games and snacks. I had to fill out paperwork to have canteen funds added to my phone account, but they lost the paperwork.

I also had to fill out paperwork to have visitors, but they kept losing that, too. Eventually I got a book. I got a Bible, too. I spent a lot of time reading the story of Esther. When I left Medicine Hat, people kept telling me I was their Esther, but I didn't really remember the story about her. It's a beautiful story about how she stood up bravely to her husband, the king, and saved her fellow Jews. Even wives weren't supposed to stand up to the king and she could have been killed for it. She risked her life to save her people.

It took them two weeks to finally sort out my paperwork so I could have visitors. Eventually, Dwayne was able to come. I don't know if they were this disorganized on purpose. I don't think they care. Why would they give a crap about the rights of prisoners? No one told them that's their job. Prison was just another example of the faceless banality of state cruelty. At one point, they took away my laundry and when it came back, my second pair of pants were missing. It took me a week to get my pants back.

The prison guards were generally decent people, though, and I tried to show them the respect they deserved. At least they were much friendlier than the police who had first arrested me and threw me in that holding cell, who were a real bunch of assholes. The two ladies who did my intake at the prison were sweet, and I thanked them for being so kind to me, after the way the police had treated me.

When the guards were taking me up to the cell block from solitary confinement, one of them even asked his colleagues, "If I tell you that I agree with what this lady did, are you going to suspend me?" At another point, a different guard just came out and told me he supported what we were doing.

You would be surprised at how many people who work for the government or the police or the justice system have privately said stuff like that to us. After he testified at the Emergencies Act inquiry, Chris Barber told me how he was out for dinner and he ran into a couple of the lawyers who had been representing the government — Justin Trudeau's government. And one of them came up to Chris and shook his hand and said, "Thanks for what you guys did."

After a week in cell block, they moved me into the dorms. Before I went, a couple of correctional officers who handle more high-profile prisoners asked to see me. They wanted to warn me that people in there can have strong views about other prisoners. If the girls don't like you, then one night one of them will just call out your name and you'll get "bounced," which is what they call getting attacked by a group of inmates. They wanted to know if I was worried about that. I told them I hadn't been, but now after talking to them, I wasn't so sure.

It was fine, though. Nobody bothered me. There was a woman there who was also arrested at the protest. One day I overheard her talking about me to some other prisoners, and I just wanted to eavesdrop and hear what they were saying, and they were talking about how my husband had been flown out to Ottawa on a private plane, which I guess really impressed them. They recognized me and I introduced myself.

Another girl there had been picked up on an arrest warrant while she was at Canadian Tire buying some supplies to help out the truckers. She told me her mom was a huge fan of mine and her dad had come up to see me speak on Parliament Hill.

One older lady who was in there with me for just a day before she left looked me in my eyes and said, "You don't belong here."

On March 3, I had been imprisoned for 14 days when Diane finally got me a bail review, which is where a Superior Court judge can review your original bail hearing for errors. This was Justice John Johnston and he was much more professional and knowledgeable than Judge Bourgeois.

Diane thought we should raise an application for apprehension of bias, because of Bourgeois' ties to the Liberal party. Karimjee went nuts about that. The idea that a big Liberal party supporter might be biased was not something that a big Liberal party supporter like himself was going to tolerate. He called it "a baseless, vexatious, frivolous and unfounded allegation made by Ms. Lich, who has consistently demonstrated that the ends justify the means."[205] The guy was out for blood.

Judge Johnston didn't seem to pay any of that much mind. He focused on our new bail application, where we proposed my sister, Dannette, as my surety, instead of my husband Dwayne. She was cross-examined. I was cross-examined. The judge seemed very impressed with my sister. He said he would deliver his ruling in a few days. I went back to prison.

On March 7, I had spent 18 days behind bars when I got the news that I was being released on bail.

I won't say I was freed, because I wasn't.

As part of the bail conditions, Dannette had to offer $20,000 in security. I was told I could not contact "either directly or indirectly, by any physical, electronic or other means" Chris Barber, Benjamin Dichter, Tom Marazzo or Danny Bulford, among other people, unless it was through lawyers or in the presence of lawyers. I was ordered not to "log on to social media or post any messages on social media."

205 https://ottawacitizen.com/news/accusations-of-judicial-bias-raised-during-tamara-lich-bail-review-hearing

Dannette would be in charge of regularly checking my phone and laptop to make sure I complied. I was ordered not to be a part of or even endorse a public protest. And I was banned from Ottawa. The judge gave me 24 hours to get out of the city and 72 hours to get out of the province.

If I did any of it, my bail would be revoked, and I would be put back in prison.

After weeks of fighting for Canadians' rights and freedoms, I was losing so many of mine. I lost my right to freedom of speech. I lost the right to be with, or even talk to my friends. After all we had been through together, we couldn't even sit down and talk about what had happened, to decompress, to share our stories and our pain. I've heard that things have gotten really bad for Tom Marazzo, and he's really struggling, but I can't reach out and help him. The saddest, hardest thing is that the people that really need each other the most right now, because we all went through the same experience, and we're all living with the aftermath, can't talk to each other. Or even just hug each other.

I have to be careful not to express any support for dissent or protest. If there are more lockdowns or mandates, I've been ordered to keep quiet about it. There are people out there, not just Karimjee, who are waiting for the chance to get me locked up again.

I had one day to get out of Ottawa and three days to get out of the province. I couldn't fly because they weren't allowing unvaccinated people on planes. I asked Dwayne to look after collecting all our stuff, which he'd left in different spots around Ottawa at people's houses, and collecting my personal effects from the prison.

He dropped me at the Swiss Hotel, where we were planning to stay that night. After I had been arrested, police had attacked the protest camp and started beating up people and rounding up other protesters, until everyone was either arrested or had left town. So there weren't many people left. I had heard about it all from prison and I was horrified. It was disgusting the violent way police handled peaceful protesters who didn't even resist them. They used pepper spray and stun grenades, and police horses trampled on an elderly woman with a walker.

Thomas O'Connor, the paramedic who lived near Ottawa, was waiting for me at the Swiss Hotel. So was Sean Tiessen, the road captain from B.C. Noeline and the other wonderful clan mothers from the Copper Dene First Nation in Yellowknife were still there too. The out-of-towners were packing up and heading out of town soon. That was supposed to be my plan, too.

But for some reason they insisted I meet this other guy who had been waiting there for me. His name was Alex and I think he was Russian. I don't know his last name, who brought him there or how he got there. He was wearing a big gold watch and gold chains and wearing a fancy suit. He looked like one of those Russian oligarchs. He told me he was friends with Donald Trump and that Trump had asked him how I was doing. Alex said he had a million dollars he was going to use to help me and that he had a private plane and would fly me home, or anywhere in the world if I wanted to flee somewhere to get asylum.

Alex ordered dinner for everyone. The whole time I'm thinking: this is beyond crazy. I mean, a Russian? Really? After all the lies that have been spread about the Freedom Convoy being controlled by foreign agents and funded by Vladimir Putin or whatever, and I just got out of prison after nearly three weeks and they're talking about putting me on the private plane of some kind of Russian oligarch who is talking about a million dollars? I didn't want to leave the country. I didn't want to fly on his plane. I just wanted to go home.

I was busting with anxiety. Time was ticking. I needed to get moving. I didn't want to stay at the Swiss Hotel after that. I said I needed to get out of there. So Sean brought me outside the hotel where they had a truck that would take me from the hotel to spend the night at Thomas's house near Ottawa, so I could start heading back west in the morning.

I took a look at this truck and my jaw dropped. It was covered in all kinds of protest signs about COVID and freedoms and it was draped in Canadian flags. I said to Sean, "I can't get in that truck. If I get in that truck, I'm going back to jail." I just couldn't figure out what these people were thinking. And Sean tells me that as long as I say I don't condone the truck, then I'll be fine.

I had no choice. I had to get going. I needed to get away from the Russian. I needed to get out of downtown Ottawa. We went out to Thomas's house in Arnprior, and Thomas and John Scubik sensed my anxiety and removed the signs from the truck early the next morning.

It took me 71 hours to get out of Ontario. We had truck trouble in Nipigon, near Thunder Bay, so we had to spend the night there. Then the next day we hit bad weather along the north tip of Lake Superior. Thank goodness I had passed on the Russian's plane offer: the clan mothers had arranged to fly back west on his jet, but then it ended up that he had plane trouble and they had to drive, and they were four hours behind me. So I wouldn't have made it if I'd stayed with them. I had to stay in touch with Det. Benson and let him know how I was progressing in terms of getting out of Ontario. I had to be out of the province by 5:30 p.m. on March 10. When we hit the Manitoba border, I texted him to say I was out.

It was 4:30 p.m. I had made it with just one hour to spare.

When I rolled into Medicine Hat a couple days later, there was a welcoming party on the highway to greet me as I came into town. They had Canadian flags, and I had to call Diane, my lawyer, to make sure it was OK for me to be seen there, that I wouldn't be violating my bail conditions if it looked like it was part of the protest or something. Diane was a bit worried. They made sure there were no signs about COVID or anything like that. When I got out to take a photo with them, instead of saying "cheese" we all said "freedom," and I immediately started to worry that I shouldn't have said that.

The first week after I got home, I took a few more days off work and I just rested. My sister had set up a postal box for me for people to send me letters and cards, and I started to go through them. There were hundreds of them, from all over the world. People wrote to me from across Canada, from the U.S., Poland, the Netherlands, Sweden and Norway. I've been working my way through them. I wanted to read every last one of them. One person sent me a Canadian flag with the words "Tamara Lich, National Hero" printed on it. One woman from Dawson Creek, B.C. made me a quilt with the words "Freedom Convoy 2022" stitched into it. I love quilts.

One woman who wrote to me was a Canadian that had been stuck in Thailand since the beginning of the pandemic. Her kids were in Canada and she hadn't seen them in over two years. She makes jewelry and she sent me a beautiful pendant with an image of a truck and the words "Canada Freedom" etched into it, along with a letter telling me her story. I reached out to her and she asked me to take a photo of me wearing the pendant and email it to her, so I did.

I'm still working on writing everyone back. We had cards printed up with a black-and-white photo of me from the convoy, in front of a Canadian flag, and there's a quote from the Bible printed in there: "'For I know the plans I have for you,' declares the Lord, 'plans to prosper you and not to harm you, plans to give you hope and a future'," Jeremiah 29:11. The card was supposed to save me time, because I was supposed to just sign it with a "thank you" and send it to people who had written me letters. But I didn't want to just do that. I've been writing my own personal responses. It's taking me a lot longer, but I'm making progress. I'm going to write everyone back.

I didn't know what it would be like when I got home to Medicine Hat. I didn't know if my house would be covered in graffiti or broken eggs, or what. With the exception of a few dirty looks at the grocery story, I've only had support. I met a man who moved to Medicine Hat from Victoria, B.C. all because this is where I'm from. Our local provincial member of the legislature, Drew Barnes, took me for coffee. He had been giving me his support through the whole thing and even wrote some articles in my defence. He reassured me I had a lot of support in the community and not to worry. He said that people in Medicine Hat would look out for me and protect me.

For two months, my life had been in a hurricane, from when I first watched Chris Barber's TikTok video to getting released from prison. It finally seemed like things would be quieting down.

And they did. For a little while.

Then, on Monday, June 27, 2022, 112 days after I walked out of that Ottawa prison, they came to arrest me again.

CHAPTER 10:

INVICTUS

The good thing about knowing a lot of truckers is it's never too long before one of them is passing through town.

In the spring of 2022, I was back at work at STEP Energy. I wasn't allowed to communicate with several of my fellow organizers without a lawyer present, due to my bail conditions. Chris Barber had similar conditions. We had set up an online group chat with our lawyers so we could talk about our cases, but it wasn't a place for much real conversation.

I was only allowed to look at Twitter, TikTok and Facebook if other people shared their screens with me. I wasn't allowed to log on or use it myself. Definitely no more Facebook Live videos. I was cut off from my people.

My office was pretty close to the Trans-Canada Highway, though, so I was never too far from a trucker. People passing by Medicine Hat who had been with us in Ottawa would stop in and see me. Some of the road captains would stop and we'd have a coffee. People would call me up and tell me that a trucker I'd never met was passing through town who just wanted to say hi and thank me.

And sometimes I would watch trucks pass by on the highway with Canadian flags waving off the back and I knew they were with us.

The Justice Centre for Constitutional Freedoms (JCCF) asked if they could honour me with their annual George Jonas Freedom Award. I didn't know much about George Jonas, to be honest. I had to look him up. He had been an author, poet and journalist who escaped Communist Hungary after the Soviets put down the 1956 revolution there. He came to Canada and wrote beautifully about freedom, most recently as a columnist in the National Post, before he died in 2016. Previous George Jonas Freedom Award recipients were former National Post journalists Mark Steyn and the late, great Christie Blatchford, and most recently the award had been given to "Canadians resisting unconstitutional lockdowns."

Of course I was touched and honoured to even be considered being included in such distinguished company. Actually, when I opened the email invitation from JCCF and saw Christie Blatchford's name, I burst into tears, because she was a hero of mine. She was such an amazing journalist and I had loved her tenacity and her brutal honesty.

There was going to be one gala dinner in Toronto in June and one in Calgary in August and they wanted me to give speeches at both of them. "Ms. Lich inspired Canadians to exercise their Charter rights and freedoms by participating actively in the democratic process, and took the initiative to help organize a peaceful protest and serve as one of its leaders," the JCCF wrote on its website when it announced I'd be getting the award. "The resulting peaceful protest in Ottawa awakened many Canadians to the injustice of Charter-violating lockdowns and mandatory vaccination policies. Ms. Lich has suffered for the cause of freedom by spending 18 days unjustly jailed, and exemplifies courage, determination and perseverance."

Rex Murphy from the National Post was going to be introducing me at the Toronto event. He's another one of my heroes and he has always been a huge defender of freedom, and had written powerful columns supporting the convoy. When Rex called me to go over our notes for our speeches, I was so excited to get to talk to him I was jumping around like a little kid at Christmas.

But Moiz Karimjee, the Crown prosecutor, was going to do everything he could to stop me from going. My bail conditions already prohibited me from going to Ontario. Those were also going to be a problem because one of my daughters was going to go to university in Ottawa in the fall, and I wanted to help get her set up.

I had switched criminal defence lawyers since my release from prison, from Diane Magas to Lawrence Greenspon, one of the country's top civil liberties lawyers. When he applied to the court to relax my conditions in May, Karimjee fought him. Not only did Karimjee want to stop me from accepting the Freedom Award, he decided to try and put me back in jail.

There was a court hearing, and I had to testify over video link from my house in Medicine Hat. Dannette had to Zoom in to testify, too, since she was my surety. My lawyer was going to make the case that since the convoy was done and the protest had dispersed, the conditions barring me from Ontario and Ottawa were too broad. And besides, I had been behaving and living a quiet life since I had been released from prison two months earlier.

Except Karimjee told the court that simply by agreeing to accept the award I had violated my bail conditions, because I was supporting the protest. He also started attacking my lawyer, Lawrence, and the JCCF. He was making accusations about the JCCF paying my legal bill and that it was funnelling money to the Freedom Convoy (which didn't even exist anymore). He was being so obnoxious even the judge seemed stunned. Lawrence objected to the whole line of attack, because my legal bills are part of solicitor-client privilege. It was shocking for Karimjee to even make these accusations.

Then Karimjee announced that he had some new and supposedly explosive evidence that was going to prove that I had violated my bail and I should be locked up again.

It was the photo of me wearing that "Freedom Canada" truck pendant that the woman in Thailand had sent me. I had emailed her the photo of me wearing it, and she posted it on social media. She had asked me if she could, and I had told her "I cannot advise you to post it or not to post it. That would go against my bail conditions. But what I will say is that people have taken pictures with me and posted it to their social media." So she posted it.

And now Karimjee was claiming this was evidence of me using social media in violation of my bail conditions.

When he cross-examined me, Karimjee asked me if by accepting the award, and appearing in a photo with the pendant, wasn't I continuing to support the convoy? I said there was no convoy to support! All the protesters had left months ago! I explained that the award was being given to me for inspiring Canadians to hold the government to account to the rule of law and to uphold their Charter rights.

Thankfully, Justice Kevin Phillips of the Ontario Superior Court agreed. In fact, he went further and smacked down Karimjee for going after me for my support of the convoy. He reminded Karimjee that bail conditions are meant to regulate behaviour, not opinions: "No court would ever seek to control the possession or manifestation of political views," he wrote in his decision. "The courts are not a thought police. We seek only to control conduct to the extent that certain behaviour will violate or likely lead to violation of the law."

The judge figured that since the protest had dispersed and there was no longer a convoy, the conditions requiring me to stay out of Ontario and Ottawa were unreasonable. I would still have to stay away from the downtown area near Parliament Hill, unless it was to attend court or meet with lawyers. But other than that, I was free to go wherever I wanted to.

Karimjee had lost again. I think it only made him madder.

Dwayne and I left Medicine Hat for Ontario about a week before the JCCF Freedom Award event and planned to stop along the way to visit some people we had met from the convoy. We were fully prepared to be pulled over along the way for some kind of minor safety violation, a broken turn signal or some trumped-up infraction. We figured Karimjee would do whatever he could to get me picked up before I made it to the JCCF dinner.

Imagine our shock that we made it all the way to Toronto without any trouble. It was a wonderful drive. People were so friendly and Ontario is such a beautiful province. I didn't get to appreciate that as much on our first drive out in January. One guy we met at the convoy lived on Manatoulin Island, and we detoured about five hours off our route just to visit him. We had left ourselves plenty of time, and it was worth it. I mean, how cool is Manatoulin Island? We fell in love with Ontario on that drive.

The dinner was scheduled for the evening of June 16 at Toronto's Eglinton Grand Theatre. We stayed the night before in Arnprior with Thomas O'Connor and drove in the day of the event. In Toronto, we stopped at the house of a woman named Stacey Kauder who we knew from the protest.

Stacey had shown up at the Swiss Hotel when I was there, and told me she was the assistant to Danny Bulford, but that ended up being a bit of an exaggeration. We got along really well. She's just a tiny little thing, but very high energy. She lived just a couple of blocks from the Eglinton Grand, and when she heard about the award she had reached out to let us use her place to get ready on the evening of the gala. And then she came along to the event with us. That ended up having consequences, to say the least.

As soon as we arrived at the Eglinton Grand, Thomas started freaking out. He had spotted Tom Marazzo. My bail conditions had specifically forbid me from communicating or contacting Tom. Thomas marched up to John Carpay, president of the JCCF, and demanded to know what the hell was going on. He reminded John that Tom Marazzo was on my no-contact list. "This guy can't be here," he said.

John said there was nothing to worry about because he was a lawyer, and he was going to be with me all night. My most recent bail conditions[206] issued by Justice Kevin Phillips said I couldn't communicate with Tom "except through counsel or in the presence of counsel." John said he would be sitting with me at the head table, so I would always be with a lawyer. I went to sit at my table, and John was there, and so was Jonathan Allen, the JCCF chairman, as well as Rex Murphy, Maxime Bernier and Rupa Subramanya, a National Post columnist who had covered the Ottawa protest and done heroic work destroying the lies that were being spread about us by Trudeau and his loyal supporters at other media outlets.

And Tom Marazzo was sitting there, too.

I thought it was strange, but I had to assume that meant everything would be fine. I mean, they wouldn't sit me right at the same table with Tom Marazzo if they thought it would end up with me being sent back to jail. Right?

Rex Murphy introduced me. He was brilliant and hilarious, of course. Rex is the king of sarcasm.

I got up and read my speech. Here's how I started:

Before I begin, I want to tell you all that I am very grateful to be here. The JCCF has become a beacon of light and a source of hope in Canada.

This award is an honour, and we must encourage and support all the men and women who bravely defend our civil liberties.

It is furthermore a great privilege to share this stage with an iconic Canadian thinker, and to receive an award named after a great novelist.

These two men — Rex Murphy and the late George Jonas — alive and in death, are two legendary torch-bearers of freedom, who are handing us a great responsibility.

It is lastly an immense honour to be here with you, those Canadians without recognizable names, who hold up this country without award

206 https://www.jccf.ca/wp-content/uploads/2022/05/R.-v.-Lich-Bail-Review-Decision-May-25-2022.pdf

and without ceremony. We must foremost be grateful to you, because you are our greatest hope. You defend our freedom.

And that is why I am here today, to talk about freedom. Because I apparently have something to do with that f-word, which has terrified our leaders.

Unfortunately, this is no simple task. The word "freedom" has become so muddied by — let's not call them the mainstream media, who are no longer mainstream, but by the mendacious media — yes, the mendacious media, who have made the term freedom synonymous with ignorance or selfishness.

The answer to the question, "what is freedom?" itself is further complicated by who you ask. There is even difference in my family:

If I ask my daughter who is a nurse, "what is freedom?" she might say, it's being off her feet, relaxing by the pool, in loungewear instead of scrubs.

If I were to ask my youngest, when she was just a little girl, freedom would have been eating ice cream before dinner.

And, if you ask my lawyer, he will tell you about the Canadian Charter of Rights and Freedoms, how bills become laws, and he might list for you some 32 sections and what they mean.

When it comes to freedom, everyone speaks their own language. People either point to what they want with freedom, or how they relate to it.

But people start to give very similar answers when freedom is taken away. For example:

People know that freedom is not being confined between four immovable walls, or else facing the punishment of more confinement. That is prison.

People know that freedom is not having your consent taken away on a whim of soulless politicians and faceless bureaucrats. That is tyranny.

People know that freedom is not being told what to think, what to say, what to believe, or else be considered too dangerous for the public hygiene. That is hell.

The idea of freedom, pursuing this line of thought, becomes a little clearer.

Let me give also you a personal description of what is not freedom: Freedom is not being arrested on a dark and deserted street, handcuffed, and searched outside in the bitter cold and snow.

Freedom is not sleeping on concrete slab without a blanket or a pillow in wet clothes, then being thrown in solitary confinement for four whole days without access to the fresh air, or books, or a telephone to contact loved ones.

Freedom is not having your paperwork lost, mysteriously, over and over again, so that for 18 days you cannot see your husband, only because of "crimes."

This may seem like an extremely unique experience.

But it's not.

All over the world, imprisonment of political free-thinkers is the norm, not the exception.

And I am very sorry to say that my experience is only a preview of what will come if we do not stand up, with a straight back, heels firmly in the soil, and unite to uphold our Charter of Rights and Freedoms.

That's just part of my speech, but it certainly seemed to resonate with the audience. At the end of the evening, I was mobbed by people, thanking me, handing me cards, taking photos with me. John Skubic was there.

After shaking hands and hugging what must have been hundreds of people, we were heading toward the exits to call it a night. I was walking with Thomas, John Carpay and another one of the JCCF lawyers, and Stacey. Tom Marazzo was nearby, too. And Stacey said, "Let's take a picture."

We went along with it.

We drove that night back all the way back to Arnprior. The next day, I woke up, looked at Dwayne's Facebook feed, and there was the photo. Online. Shared with the world. Stacey had posted it. You could see me and Tom Marazzo. The lawyers were standing just outside the frame.

I still cannot figure out for the life of me what Stacey was thinking. We messaged her and told her to take it down. John messaged her as well asking her to take it down. People commented on the photo telling Stacey she was going to get me in trouble, and she would give stupid responses like "you hate freedom." Thomas asked her to take it down. She never did. I think it was just a way for her to say, "Hey, look who I know," and to see how many likes she could get on her Facebook page. Even if she had taken it down, I wasn't convinced there wouldn't be repercussions. I was sure someone would have taken a screenshot of it and Karimjee would see it soon enough. I was right.

I called Dannette, as my surety, and I sent her the picture and let her know what happened. I explained how there were lawyers standing all around us. But I couldn't shake the anxiety I was feeling. I couldn't be sure there wouldn't be trouble. We drove home to Medicine Hat. A couple of weeks went by and nothing happened. I gradually stopped worrying about it.

On Monday June 27, 11 days after that photo was taken, I left work. I stopped at Dannette's house so she could look at my phone and make sure I was keeping to my bail conditions. I picked up the latest batch of fan mail from her. We visited for a little bit. Then I drove home.

I was a couple of blocks away from my house, when I saw flashing police lights in my rear-view mirror.

I've had a few speeding tickets in my day. They're kind of a thing for me. I thought, "Oh crap, he must have clocked me speeding." I pulled over and got my licence, insurance and registration ready. The officer walked up to my window. I rolled it down and put on my cheeriest voice and said, "Good afternoon. I've got everything here ready for you." And I tried to hand him my licence.

He didn't even glance at it. He just said, "Ma'am when I run your plates, it's coming back that there's a warrant for your arrest."

I was stunned. I asked if he was kidding. He said no. I asked him if I could take my truck home and drop it off there, since it was just around the corner, and he said no. But he said I could text my husband and tell him what was happening and that he needed to come get the truck. I texted Dwayne and then left my phone in the truck.

It seemed to me like this officer would have rather been doing anything else than this. He seemed so uncomfortable. I asked him his name, and he said it was Josh. He looked like he was still in his twenties. He cuffed me and put me in the cruiser and drove me to the station. I spent the night in a holding cell. This time, they gave me a blanket.

I found out later that Karimjee had been working on a Canada-wide warrant for days before that, and that he even had the police in Medicine Hat put me under surveillance. If he had just called my lawyer, I would have turned myself in. There was no need for all that effort, and expense. But Karimjee seems to enjoy theatrics.

Karimjee had two pieces of evidence that he claimed were proof of me violating my bail conditions. One was the photo from the gala.

Brigitte Belton had sent it to him. She wanted me back in jail so badly, that she publicly bragged about turning me in.

The other piece of evidence was a short video from the same gala that someone in the audience had taken and posted on his Facebook page. It showed me coming back to my table after the speech. Tom Marazzo had congratulated me on my speech, and I had said "thank you" to him and I guess I tapped him on the shoulder or gave it a squeeze or something. That was it. In the video, you could even see John Carpay, a lawyer, sitting at the table.

The next day, Tuesday, they took me to the remand centre, where I was strip-searched and had to change into a prison uniform. There was a quick hearing that night by video, and the court gave the Ottawa cops six days to come get me, or I would be released.

They didn't need six days. They came right away.

On Wednesday, they cuffed me and shackled my legs and drove me to Calgary, where I was going to be picked up by Det. Benson, who was going to fly me back to Ottawa that night. As they were getting me ready for the transport to Calgary, one officer came over to me and thanked me, saying that we had helped to give a future to his kids. "There's a lot of us behind you," he said. "Stay strong."

They had me change into my street clothes again. When I was arrested, I was wearing a hoodie that a friend had given me that was from a convoy protest in B.C. in March called The Great Canadian Cruise. Down the arm of this hoodie it says in big white block letters "HOLD THE LINE." And on the other arm it says ""FREEDOM CANNONS." And over the heart, it says "Freedom Over Fear." So that's what I would be wearing to Ottawa, and that's what I would be wearing in the court hearing over my bail conditions, because they always have you change into your street clothes for the hearings. It was going to be awkward. When I was in court, I made a point of rolling up those sleeves as high as they would go. I knew that if Karimjee saw them, his head would explode.

When they got me to the Calgary airport, they loaded me into a wheelchair, I guess because I couldn't walk in the leg shackles. They rolled me into a cell at the airport, uncuffed me, and left me to wait.

I started doing push-ups and stretches, just to kill time, and then the door opened and Det. Benson walked in. He said, "Hi Tamara, how are you doing?" I said I was fine. He had come with another officer from the Ottawa Police Service, Sgt. Mahad Hassan. Sgt. Hassan was actually a really nice gentleman, and he and I had some very pleasant, fairly normal chats that evening.

Det. Benson gave me the flight details about when we would be boarding, and said they would be back to get me when it was time to go. On his way out the door, he stopped and turned to me and said "Oh, by the way, we need to wear masks on the plane. Are you going to give us a hassle?"

I told him, no. I said that I wanted this whole thing to go as smoothly as he did, and I had no problem wearing a mask.

After a little while, they came and put my shackles on again, and put me in the wheelchair. This time they left my handcuffs off. Sgt. Hassan said he wanted me to keep my dignity. They were still wheeling me through the airport in a wheelchair with leg shackles on, but whatever. At least it was something. They were also taking me to a gate that was way on the other side of the terminal. It was a long trip and I thought people in the airport would all be staring at me, but everybody's faces were stuck to their phones and I think maybe just a handful of people even glanced at me.

They took my shackles off as we boarded the plane. The best thing about the plane ride was that they let me order a coffee. I didn't know if they were going to let me have anything, but they were completely chill about it and said I could have coffee and a snack if I wanted. I knew once I got to the Ottawa detention centre there would be no real coffee — just the packet of instant they give you in the morning, and then that's it — so I knew my coffee window was rapidly closing.

It would be a long time before I would have real coffee again.

I spent that night in a holding cell at the Ottawa police station. I sat through another questioning by Det. Benson, who patiently listened to my repeated "no comments." He asked me to sign something, a paper acknowledging that I had been arrested for breaching my bail conditions, but I politely declined. Then it was back to the detention centre.

My hearing after getting back to Ottawa was from jail on the following Tuesday, nearly a week after my arrival. I was set up with a video link in the basement of the detention centre, but there were technical problems, so someone brought in a cell phone. Karimjee presented the video that showed me interacting with Tom Marazzo at the head table of the JCCF gala and the photo that Stacey had posted that Brigitte had sent to him. When Det. Benson was cross-examined, it seemed like he wasn't even trying. He answered Karimjee's questions, but he had nothing to add about the photo. He hadn't done any investigations into the circumstances of the photo. It seemed to me he wasn't really into helping Karimjee put me back in jail.

We figured we had it in the bag. My lawyer, Lawrence Greenspon, along with his partner, Eric Granger, presented convincing evidence that there were lawyers all around me at all times at the gala. Paul Harris was adjudicating the trial. Even though he was a justice of the peace, he came across as a reasonable and fair man. I later found out he had no legal background at all. He had been a purchasing agent for Parks Canada before he became a justice of the peace. The hearing took hours, because Karimjee always goes on for hours. Harris said he would deliver his decision on Friday.

When he did, he had me stand up in court while he read the charges. And Harris ripped a strip off of me. He said it was "absolutely ridiculous" that I thought it was okay to talk to Tom Marazzo just because there were lawyers there. He said that if he let me go, Ottawa's "vulnerable victims" of the Freedom Convoy would have to live in fear that the trucks would come back if I were allowed to communicate with other organizers. He kept talking about how I was facing a long prison sentence, and referring to firearm offences, which had nothing to do with my case. He told me: "Your detention is necessary to maintain confidence in the administration of justice."

I was completely shaken. I was going back to prison, apparently until my criminal trial, whenever that was going to be. I was having trouble keeping up hope after hearing Harris tear into me like that. If it hadn't been for Robert, I might have been lost. Robert was an angel sent by God that day to comfort me.

Robert was an officer who worked at the courthouse. I never got his last name. When they took me to the courthouse cell to await transport back to the detention centre, he was waiting there, at the door of the cell. And he asked if he could tell me something. He said he was from Poland, and that his whole church congregation was praying for me. He told me that where he comes from, I'm what they call a political prisoner. "I just want to thank you for everything you've done," he said.

Those few words from Robert changed everything for me that day. They gave me new strength. And later, when Robert came to get me from the cell to move me to the transport, he told me it broke his heart to put handcuffs on me. He looked at me and said, "don't give up." I promised him I wouldn't.

After he dropped me off he told me it was an honour to meet me. "We're going to keep praying for you," he said. I thanked him and promised I would pray for him, too, because he was sent from heaven that day to rescue me. I never saw him again, but I thought about Robert every day I was in prison.

I had been arrested on June 27. My lawyers would now have to arrange for me to have another hearing where a judge would review Harris's decision, which could take weeks to set up, and there was no telling how that would work out. They didn't put me in solitary this time, but sent me straight to cell block to quarantine with two other ladies. They let me have a Bible, some books and playing cards. My cellmates were a couple of schizophrenic drug addicts.

One of them, Ergine, was six months pregnant with her fifth child. The other, Kristy, slept on a mat on the floor and barely ate, but she refused to throw out her food, and she would pile it up in the corner of the cell. She said she got messages and energy from the garbage.

Both of them were prone to screaming fits. At one point, Ergine started describing in graphic detail how she was going to rape me due to her raging pregnant hormones. It was all so surreal.

After one of Ergine's more violent outbursts, one of the guards, Sgt. Frank — we called him Big Frank — came to move me and Kristy out of there to a different cell, away from Ergine. A couple of days after that, they moved the two of us from cell block to the dorms.

The first time I was in prison, in February, I didn't have much to write with. Just a few sheets of looseleaf. This time, they gave me a good supply of paper, which I kept in a bright yellow folder.

I wrote on the folder some quotes on that would give me strength. "Courage is not the absence of fear or despair, but the strength to conquer them." And Bible passages from Mark 3:24-27: "And if a house be divided against itself, that house cannot stand…no man can enter a strong man's house and spoil his goods, except he will first bind the strong man; then he will spoil his house." And from Ecclesiastes 10:16: "Woe to thee, O land, when thy king is a child and thy princes eat in the morning."

And I had written out the entire poem of Invictus, by William Ernest Henley. The title, Invictus, means unconquerable:

Out of the night that covers me,
Black as the pit from pole to pole,
I thank whatever gods may be
For my unconquerable soul.

In the fell clutch of circumstance
I have not winced nor cried aloud.
Under the bludgeonings of chance
My head is bloody, but unbowed.

Beyond this place of wrath and tears
Looms but the Horror of the shade,
And yet the menace of the years

Finds and shall find me unafraid.

It matters not how strait the gate,
How charged with punishments the scroll,
I am the master of my fate,
I am the captain of my soul.

I also kept a diary the whole time I was there. Here are some of the entries:

July 9

Phones still down and only working sporadically. Managed to get a call into Dwayne, Thomas and briefly to my sister. Ergine gone to hospital to get checked out. I was given Access — nice to have a little time alone. Morning spent reading the Bible. Trying to be strong but am a little emotional when thinking about my daughters. Thomas is going to put money on my canteen tomorrow if my visitor list has been processed. Really hoping for some yard time today, have only been outside once since arriving.

Got a shower this morning! Talked to Sgt. Frank. He is checking our quarantine status (it's up tomorrow). Not sure if I will be moved to dorms or not — I hope not, not yet anyhow, but hopefully these other two can go.

Ergine arrived back from the hospital and had an epic stage 4 meltdown. Sgt. Frank moved myself and Christy from cell #4 across the hall to cell #8. Sherry [a guard] was kind enough to give me some cleaner and I washed the graffiti off the walls again. Lol.

July 10

Morning uneventful, another terrible sleep. I wish I brought my mat over from the other cell — this one sucks. Read Mary, Queen of Scots most of the morning and some Bible reading. Sent request form in to meet with the chaplain and attend Bible study. Made myself a calendar; time can get away from you in here.

ACCESS!! Called mom, Dad, Thomas, Dwayne and Eva.

Yard! Great workout today!

Evening phone … Everyone seemed to be asleep so I was super lucky to have extra phone time this evening. … Hoping to see the Dr tomorrow for a day or two of sleeping meds to help me get at least 1 or 2 good nights sleep.

…. I have been terminated from STEP Energy. Dwayne is going to retrieve my belongings tomorrow.

July 11

Monday — did not have a great sleep again. I need a different mat. At this point I think the hard steel frame would be better. Spent my morning reading the Bible (Ezra and Job. I am really liking Job so far). Wrote my grandma. I was sent for Access about 10:45 and called Grandma for her mailing address and we had a good talk. I called Eric next for any updates. He is expecting a date for the bail review later today or tomorrow. He said they should have the transcripts from this past hearing by Wednesday and they are hoping for a hearing date for the review next week. Karimjee has agreed to keep it to one day...

Lawrence also received an email from John Carpay and [former Opposition leader] Preston Manning. In it was a link to an op-ed in the Epoch Times by Mr. Manning entitled "The Unconscionable Persecution of Tamara Lich." I can't wait to read it! I will touch base with Eric tomorrow to find out about the hearing date.

I called mom and dad and had a great visit. I joke with mom that being in jail has its perks as I get to talk to them so often. Some news from them: 17 countries have openly stated they want nothing to do with our so-called Prime Minister and if they have any dealings with Canada they will do so through Ministers of those departments only. Mom and dad also mentioned that [NDP Leader Jagmeet] Singh is losing the support of some of his MPs — let's hope Keith Wilson was right last night when he told me it looked like the love-in between Singh & Trudeau appeared to be coming to an end. Mom also mentioned that [Alberta politician] Brian Jean has come to my defence via some Facebook posts expressing his absolute shock over the Justice's decision on Friday.

Hope I get yard today.

Yard — Cardio and Burpees (x60)

...Chaplain came by today as per my request. He is going to get me a King James Bible. Bible study classes are only for the males right now and same with Sunday mass but he does have some materials he will get for me — workbook type stuff for Bible study.

July 12

Christy and I were taken off quarantine officially this morning. She went to dorms — I went to the dayroom with the rest of cell block. Ate lunch, called Dwayne, Eric, Thomas and mom and dad. Went back to my cell and Frank came and asked what I was doing. I told him I preferred to stay in the cell block if possible. He told me about who was about to be my new cellmate. I packed up and am now in Dorm #1. Top bunk... no shelf and I have been warned there is a thief and to keep my belongings close.

Sent in a request form to meet with the Native Liaison Officer (NILO).

...No yard today — Dorm went out early this morning It's ok, I have been working out everyday so a rest day isn't terrible.

...Also [former Opposition leaders] Stockwell Day, Preston Manning and some other notable people are planning to do a live Twitter Spaces to discuss my case.

July 13

WOKE UP — COFFEE — WORKOUT!

My canteen order did not come last night... Prepared canteen order for today. Hoping to get to the yard today to run.

Called Eric, they just received word of a possible review date of July 25. The judge is from out of town, he thinks the Hamilton area, he has a criminal background and hasn't been hesitant to release people on bail in the past. Even according to JP Harris, Dannette is still a good surety. With regards to the bail review dates, it also looks like they will have a spillover date of July 27 if we don't finish up on the 25th. Good news as we could have a decision that day then.

When I got off the phone I noticed Kristy was gone. Girls had her removed from dorms due to her obsession with keeping and collecting her garbage (she told me she receives energy and messages from her food garbage). Good news for me, I now have a bottom bunk and two mats!

Read more of the Mary bio…Called Dwayne — he's at the farm with his brother, took the cats and the kittens. I'm so sad I didn't get to watch them grow.

Called mom too — one big perk about jail is talking to my parents every day. They are so supportive and we always share a laugh and occasionally tears.

Called Eva, she is going to forward Brigitte's videos to Lawrence and Eric and suggested someone send them to Karimjee. That may, perhaps, grant Brigitte her greatest wish…

Rest of the night was uneventful. I played a little solitaire, started my Bible study course and read a little more.

July 14

Helped clean dorm this morning, also forgot to mention yesterday I applied for a job in the laundry department, best to stay busy. Yard just after meds this morning, ran, walked, 70 burpees, had to outdo my 60 from the other day. Read some Bible in the am…

Called Susan (from my phone messages). She is a supporter and so thrilled I called her back. We had a lovely chat. What can we do out here? she asked. Be kind to each other, that's how we win this I told her. You have said that all along, she said. Thanked her for her support, love and prayers.

Sent request form to change my PIN. I think Ergine has it and is using it. (Done).

Phone call rundown: Called Eric, confirmed dates for bail review and they will be July 25 & 27. Doesn't sound like Dee [Danette] or I will have to be put on the stand.

...Another terrible sleep!

July 15

I have now been in jail for the same amount of days as I was in the winter and still have at least 2 weeks to go. Spent some time this morning reading Matthew, committed some time to memorizing Invictus, went to yard around 10:30 and did my strength workout — sucks we only have 20 minutes.

July 16

Spent the morning reading the Bible, finished Matthew and most of Mark. Melissa [the pastor from the Biker's Church] came to visit me today. It was lovely to see her. She said Pat [King] is doing ok and his decision from his hearing this last week will come Monday morning. I am praying for his release.

She told me I have so much support. I told her I am doing well and that I am taking good care of myself. Called Thomas after lunch.

Yard — workout was a little sluggish but I got a short run in, 40 burpees, pulled left oblique so switched to mountain climbers. Spent evening playing Sequence and cards, had a decent sleep.

July 17

Morning spent reading the Bible. Called Thomas after lunch. William has a job offer for me. Thomas will have him prepare a description and info for me. He said this could possibly be a way to have most of my conditions dropped and said there is existing case law for this.

...Called Dwayne, was able to get through finally.

The convoy, jail, all of it has forever changed my life. God only knows if I will be back here again or not. There are no guarantees for anything anymore. Really hoping for a positive outcome next week. The sooner I am out of here the better.

July 18

Read Mary, Queen of Scots bio most of the morning. We had yard around 10:30 — did a little light jog but I pulled an oblique a few days ago so I kept my workout light. Called Melissa at 11. She was just outside the courthouse with Christy (Pat's girlfriend). PAT IS GETTING RELEASED!!! Almost 5 months to the day of his arrest (FEB 19).

Had good chats today with mom and dad. … Eric advised today the hearing dates are now Monday and Tuesday, July 25 & 26. Thomas is coming tomorrow!

July 19

Read most of the morning. Thomas came to visit at 10:30 and brought me fresh clothes. He said Alberta has dropped all of their vax mandates! For everything!! He also chatted about me and Dwayne's situation. Also discussed William's job offer which sounds pretty amazing … I will discuss it with my legal team although working with mom and dad is also extremely appealing. We also discussed Pat's conditions; deletion of all social media, curfew, live with his surety, etc. Most of them so harsh! Thomas also said Melissa came yesterday and put $180 on my canteen account…

July 20

Shower, laundry, chatted with Tamara. Yard and strength workout. Called Eric and discussed job offer — best to wait — I am to call Lawrence at 11 am…

Called dad, he just watched a video (live) of MEP Christine Anderson sign papers for my formal nomination for a Nobel Peace Prize in the EU…

July 21

Breakfast was 2 ½ hours late. Kitchen staff had been sent home, apparently due to with exposure to covid....HA HA HA HA HA! Happy surprise — Melissa came to visit me... Melissa also told me that there was an Aaron [Erin] here who was the man at the convoy who never wore a shirt — he has been here since April (Biker Rally). She found out he was here while visiting Pat. I am going to get more info and maybe we can help him. Called Eva after lunch and let her know. Will call Melissa later and get more info on him Eva also mentioned Brian Peckford has confirmed he will be attending the awards dinner in Calgary...

Called Thomas... We are going to try to get to Montreal Tuesday if I am out early enough. If not then Wednesday. Also he said to call Melissa.

Melissa — she forgot to tell me she is going to the cabin Sunday for a few days and also that she put $120 on my canteen. I thanked her. She gave me some info on Erin Aldrich [the biker]. He was arrested as a result of Rolling Thunder in April...She is going to find out his lawyers name, what his charges are and if he has any bail hearings or appearances coming up. I asked Melissa to pass on my number and we will get him some help. She mentioned to me in our visit today that he has no help, no money, no family and no way home.

More drama with Brigitte, she was on Tiktok saying convoy bought a church and that when I got back from Ottawa in the winter I bought a new truck and also that Chad, Sean and I were talking about buying a building by the Swiss. Totally crazy talk and bold faced lies. Up until now we have been ignoring her but this is getting ridiculous.

July 22

literally too much to write about...

July 23

......seriously sometimes too much going on. My head is full.

July 24

No yard today. No yard yesterday. Nicola said we are on lockdown because they are short staffed.

Quiet Sunday... Mentally preparing for what to get ready for tomorrow. Although I do not anticipate being released tomorrow I am packing up as if I am just in case. Gave some things to Peng and will leave my shampoo with Crystal to give to her in case I don't come back. Want to leave my toothpaste for Dana too Other than those items I am not concerned with the rest of it. I am planning to spend a few days here possibly at Thomas & leigh-anne's cabin to take some time for myself and decompress a bit, especially after this crazy week. Will call Dee after supper and probably Dwayne, tried Eva a couple of times earlier as I wanted to get Ryan O's number.

That was the last entry in my jail diary. On July 25, I would be appearing before Ontario Superior Court Justice Andrew Goodman for a bail review.

It would be nothing like what I had expected.

CHAPTER 11:

WHAT WE EXPOSED

Karimjee was obviously desperate to keep me in prison. My bail review was scheduled over two days, July 25 and 26. It was intended to be strictly a review of the Harris decision, where the judge would decide whether the justice of the peace had made an error in administering the law.

I was prepared for the worst. I never seemed to have normal bail hearings. I knew it would be two days of Karimjee ranting on and on about what a menace I was, how serious the charges were and how I needed to be kept behind bars. Then I would probably have to wait in prison for several days while the judge weighed his decision.

Ontario Superior Court Justice Andrew Goodman had something else in store.

My lawyers, Lawrence and Eric, explained to the judge everything that was wrong in the decision where Harris had revoked my bail. They presented evidence that I had barely interacted with Tom Marazzo at the gala.

And they argued that I had now spent 48 days in prison, which was probably more than I would ever serve if I was actually convicted of mischief.

Karimjee refused to accept that. He insisted I could be serving a lengthy sentence, and that I was facing 10 years in prison. He liked to compare the maximum sentence to a firearms offence, which was also punishable by 10 years in prison. He was always bringing up firearms, I think as a way to try and paint me as violent and dangerous. He needed to make it seem that a mischief charge, which is usually filed for minor offences, was a big, scary deal in my case.

Karimjee was cherry-picking the Criminal Code[207], anyway. There are different kinds of mischief, from vandalism to computer hacking to endangering life. It's true that the maximum sentence for the more serious kinds of mischief is 10 years. But for more typical mischief, the maximum is two years, and judges will give as little jail time as they consider appropriate, or no jail time at all, which is common.

Goodman asked Karimjee if he had ever found evidence of a single mischief case that had even come close to resulting in 10 years in prison.

Karimjee had to admit that, no, he hadn't. But then he said that was because there had never been a mischief charge in the whole history of Canada that was as serious as mine, because our protest had been so disruptive. "If not in a situation such as this, then what other situation?" he said.

Karimjee's strategy had backfired. He had made a big deal of the 10-year sentence and when the judge called him on his crap, he had nothing to back it up.

By Monday afternoon, Goodman had heard enough. He said he had found errors in the Harris decision, and said that Harris's inflammatory statements about the "ridiculous" interpretation of my bail conditions had "compounded" the errors. Goodman decided my interactions with Tom Marazzo were "tenuous." He not only set aside the original bail decision from two weeks earlier, he ordered a whole new bail review for me, a "de novo" review, that would occur the next day.

Karimjee had lost again.

---

207 https://laws-lois.justice.gc.ca/eng/acts/c-46/section-430.html

Karimjee seemed to only win when he was dealing with justices of the peace, who didn't really know the law. Whenever he came up against real judges, he couldn't convince them of his case.

I don't know all the reasons Goodman ordered a "de novo" review. I guess he made it seem like I had been out on bail long enough, since March 7, that it was time to revisit the original conditions they had put on me when back when they didn't know if I would behave myself or not. But I wonder if he also thought that I had been through enough.

On the second day, the day of the "de novo" review, Karimjee announced to the court yet again that he had new evidence that would prove that I had violated my bail conditions. He hadn't disclosed this new evidence to defence, which the Crown has to do so the other side can prepare for it. My lawyers objected. It was more dirty tricks from Karimjee. But judges give a lot of latitude to Crown attorneys, and Goodman said he would hear it.

I was racking my brain trying to figure out what this explosive new evidence was. Had someone recorded me having a private conversation? Had Karimjee tapped my phone and caught me accidentally admitting that I was proud of the truckers, or that I thought Trudeau was a terrible prime minister or something? I had been in prison for so long, and I really, really didn't want to go back. I missed my home and my family so much. I was sick to my stomach, waiting for this bombshell. But I realized there was nothing I could do but pray, and give it over to God.

All it was was a TikTok video from Brigitte Belton accusing me of taking the money we raised in the Freedom Convoy and claiming I was trying to use it to buy an old, unused church property in Ottawa. She had posted it a few days earlier. I had learned about it when I was in prison, and mentioned it in my prison diary. Brigitte had been accusing me and other organizers of embezzling money from the Freedom Convoy, and she was spreading lies about how we were buying things like new trucks and buying this church and other properties. It was all nonsense. When I saw that Karimjee's so-called evidence was just this angry lady on TikTok making loony claims with no proof, I was so relieved! I thought, "I got this."

It is true that some of the Freedom Convoy protesters had set up a group called The United People of Canada and were trying to buy the former St. Brigid's Church a few blocks from Parliament Hill. They were going to call it The United People's Church, so they could have a facility where people would have a place to gather in case there were other protest events in the future in Ottawa. They had even gotten Dwayne involved as an advisor. But I wanted nothing to do with it. And the guy behind the church plan, William Komer, had made it clear he wasn't representing the Freedom Convoy.

So, I wasn't even involved with the church deal that Brigitte was talking about. The idea of having a meeting place wasn't a bad idea, I guess. But the business with this church got kind of ridiculous. After the deal fell through[208], because The United People of Canada couldn't make the payments, and they were going to evict them, Komer set up in front of the church with a crown and tinfoil sceptre, and guards carrying squirt guns. I don't know what they were thinking. I thought it was kind of ridiculous and embarrassing, and it was making the whole freedom movement look bad.

Ever since I got out of prison, Brigitte has been trying to help Karimjee put me back in. She's so bitter about not getting the credit she thinks she deserves, that she's actually working now with the Crown prosecutor to try and get her fellow organizers put in jail. I just think it's unfortunate that one of our own family has turned against us all like this, because to me, that's what we are. That's what we became out there: a family. And so to see all these egos now, it's tough. It's really tough to watch the wonderful family we had falling apart like this.

Karimjee had presented a newspaper article about The United People of Canada and the church as evidence against me. Judge

208 https://ottawacitizen.com/news/local-news/united-people-of-canada-dig-in-at-st-brigids-as-eviction-notice-deadline-passes

Goodman was not impressed and basically decided it was a big nothing burger. At one point, he indicated towards the video of Brigitte and said, "Could you get that off the screen please?" and he tossed the article away.

I noticed that when they walked me to the stand to testify, in my leg shackles, the judge looked away — almost like he was disgusted seeing it. I wasn't sure what he was thinking. But by the end of the day, you could see how frustrated this judge was and how annoyed with Karimjee he was. After Karimjee wrapped up his summation, the judge didn't even have any questions for my lawyer. He just pulled together his notes and said, "I'm going to be back in 15 minutes with a decision."

I was shocked. I had never had a judge say they had come to a decision that quickly before. Usually it took a day or several days. Lawrence had warned me before that I would probably have to go back to the detention centre for a few days until the decision came, but after what happened he said it was a good sign. He said he suspected I was about to be released. I was so emotional, I had a bit of a breakdown. I started shaking and crying. I was afraid to get my hopes up, because I had been burned so many times before, but I couldn't help it.

And then the judge came back with his decision. It was probably the most polite bitch slap of Karimjee I could ever hope to witness. It was amazing! He said Karimjee was wrong about me facing a long prison sentence and that there was no danger in releasing me from prison. Here's an excerpt from the judgment:

"Fundamentally, Ms. Lich is charged with mischief and obstructing police-related offences, not sedition or inciting a riot… I opine that it is highly unlikely that this 49-year-old accused, with no prior criminal record and questions regarding her direct participation in the overall protests and gridlock of the city, would face a potential lengthy term of imprisonment… [T]aking the Crown's case at its very highest, the reality is that the applicant would spend very little additional time (if any) in custody than she has

already served. Again, I say this only in respect of my overall analysis for this bail review.

"In my opinion, a reasonable member of the community, informed of the principles of fundamental justice and Charter values and who appreciates the presumption of innocence and the constitutional right to reasonable bail would not view Ms. Lich's release with great shock and indignation. The proffered release plan will provide that the risk of re-offence in relation to the essential core of the alleged offences is sufficiently low and public confidence would be maintained in the administration of justice."

He had ordered my release! He increased the surety amount that me and my sister had to put up from $25,000 to $37,000, unfortunately. But then he spoke to me directly and said to me that I needed to be smart, and he didn't want to see me back in court. "You're under a microscope," he said. "And you need to be very careful."

And then he gave his order to the bailiff: "Take those shackles off."

....

I was out. For now.

But I had spent 49 days in prison and I hadn't even been convicted of a crime.

There are violent offenders in this country who have served less time than I have.

Like Mohammed Majidpour. In 2021, he was charged with criminal harassment for allegedly stalking a Vancouver woman, who recorded the incident on video. That charge was stayed, and Majidpour instead pled guilty to a variety of other charges including assault with a weapon, uttering threats, break and enter and (like me) mischief. He was sentenced to a single day in prison[209], despite having a record

209 https://globalnews.ca/news/9207826/repeat-vancouver-offender-mohammed-majidpour-arrested-again/

of 30 convictions, including violent and random attacks. Then, on September 27, 2022, he allegedly attacked a 19-year-old Asian woman in Vancouver while barking racist and other offensive comments at her. A Canada-wide warrant was put out for his arrest on October 6. After being arrested on October 10[210], he was released on bail on October 11. He was out in one day. And then he was arrested two hours later for allegedly stealing hundreds of dollars of clothing from a store.

Violent criminals in Canada will often barely see the inside of a jail cell before they're released on bail, and then they're back again, and out again, like a revolving door. The alleged murderer who stabbed a young RCMP outreach officer to death in Burnaby, B.C. on October 18, 2022 was already facing assault charges from March, but he had been released on bail — and then failed to show up to his court hearings. A year earlier, he had been arrested for assault and resisting a police officer.

B.C.'s attorney general has warned[211] that courts are too easily letting repeat and violent offenders out on bail after short jail visits. It's known as Canada's "catch and release"[212] system.

Only, when it comes to a Métis grandmother, with no criminal record at all, peacefully protesting in the nation's capital to uphold Charter freedoms, there is no catch and release. The Crown prosecutor and the judge and justices of the peace who refused to let me out on bail offered me no presumption of innocence, either. Instead of Karimjee having to prove his case against me, my lawyers were forced to prove that I was innocent of the absurd claims that Karimjee kept making that had no basis in reality.

---

210 https://www.vancouverisawesome.com/local-news/repeat-offender-vpd-vancouver-bc-5973117

211 https://bc.ctvnews.ca/violent-repeat-offenders-being-released-on-bail-due-to-unintended-consequences-b-c-attorney-general-1.6105990

212 https://www.timescolonist.com/local-news/catch-and-release-bail-changes-mean-more-accused-criminals-sent-back-into-community-4692087

When I went back to Medicine Hat, I had no job waiting for me anymore. The people at STEP Energy Services had always been very supportive of me through the whole convoy and everything. But there were a couple of gentlemen on the board of directors who were getting freaked out with my name being in the media so much. When I was arrested on June 27, that was their breaking point. I called my district manager from prison in Ottawa and he told me it was over. I was disappointed, but I believe everything happens for a reason. In my heart, I think I already knew that after all I had been through, my life was not meant to be about filling in spreadsheets and purchase orders.

I lost my job. I lost my freedom of speech. I lost my freedom to communicate with my friends. I have to be careful about every move that I make. I'm under a microscope. I'm nervous to have my 19-year-old daughter be around me in case they come to arrest me again. I don't want her to witness that. When I was in prison, she woke up and read a fake rumour spreading on the internet that I had hanged myself in my cell.

I haven't even seen the details of the mischief charge that I'm alleged to have committed. My trial isn't scheduled until late 2023, and I have to live like this until then.

When I came back to Ottawa in the fall of 2022, someone called the police when they saw me smoking outside my hotel. The cops came to warn me that I had to stay on the part of the sidewalk that was hotel property because my bail conditions banned me from downtown Ottawa unless I was with my lawyer. When I went to visit a Legion hall with one of the veterans I had met during the protest, the manager told me to leave. She said my presence there was "divisive" and "political." When I went to a different pub, I noticed a man in a suit watching me from a rooftop across the street.

I had come back to the capital for the start of the Public Order Emergency Commission on October 13, 2022. The Emergencies Act was designed to be used only in rare and extremely dangerous circumstances, and so the legislation itself says that if the prime minister uses it, it automatically triggers an inquiry "held into the circumstances that led to the declaration being issued and the measures taken for dealing with the emergency." The inquiry has to produce a report within 360 days of the Emergencies Act being revoked. The Public Order Emergency Commission has to issue its findings, determining whether the Liberal government was justified in invoking the act, by February 6, 2023.

Over six weeks of hearings, Justin Trudeau's decision to invoke the most drastic law in Canada would be on trial.

And I was damn well sure I was going to be there in Ottawa to witness it.

Of course, I was also being called to testify. So were other people who were involved in making the Freedom Convoy happen: Chris Barber, Tom Marazzo, Brigitte Belton, Benjamin Dichter, Pat King, Keith Wilson, James Bauder and Danny Bulford.

Also former Ottawa police chief Peter Sloly, current acting chief Steve Bell and Ottawa's former mayor Jim Watson, as well as some of the OPP and RCMP senior people, and some Ottawa officials and local people. Justin Trudeau was going to testify. Same with several cabinet ministers, as well as deputy ministers, senior civil servants and Trudeau's senior intelligence advisor, Jody Thomas. Ontario Premier Doug Ford and his solicitor general were asked to testify, but they refused.

In a country with real leadership, I think a premier refusing to testify at an inquiry of such historic importance would be political suicide. I think even having an inquiry like this would be fatal for a prime minister. But this isn't a country with real leadership. The Freedom Convoy exposed a lot of lies and misbeliefs. One of the things we exposed is the hollowness and cowardice of the so-called leaders of this country.

I had had my doubts about the Freedom Convoy at the start. I had seen convoys come and go before. I had been part of protests that kept holding demonstrations for years. Nothing ever changed.

This time was different. This time we had the support of hundreds of thousands of people, not just in Canada, but worldwide. This time, we had been fighting not for the economic freedoms of Western Canada, but for the fundamental human rights and freedoms of everyone. And this time, we had exposed the truth about the dangers we all face.

We exposed the Liberal-friendly mainstream media for its agenda and its lies. People across Canada, and around the world, could see how the CBC, the Toronto Star, CTV, The Globe and Mail and many others were working to vilify peaceful protesters in service to a corrupt prime minister who writes their bailout cheques. For every honest journalist — and there were some — there were a dozen or more who were out to call us Nazis or violent criminals, or claiming we were foreign agents or trying to overthrow the government.

We exposed woke Silicon Valley corporations like *GoFundMe* as being politically biased, eager to promote any left-wing campaign, even ones involving criminal activity, but totally against any cause that wasn't backed by the liberal elite.

We exposed the banking system, too. When the government ordered the banks to seize people's personal savings, their private property, all for the crime of donating a few dollars to a cause that Trudeau hated, the banks didn't hesitate in ruining people's finances and their credit. Evidence at the Emergencies Act inquiry showed that Finance Minister Chrystia Freeland had wanted anyone who had their bank accounts frozen to have to report to police to get their money back. And the banks were happy about it.[213] According to confidential cabinet minutes, "Banks were pleased that the government was working on a plan that would see individuals with their bank accounts frozen

213 https://www.blacklocks.ca/freeland-wanted-police-tabs-on-account-holders-records/

report to police prior to the bank to have their accounts unfrozen." The banks have been revealed to be part of the state's mission to control us.

We exposed the weak leadership of the Conservative party in the face of Trudeau's outrageous assault on Canadian freedoms. The day we arrived in Ottawa, the leader of the federal Conservative party was Erin O'Toole, who did not support the convoy. Three days later[214], he was pushed out by his caucus. The new Conservative leader, Pierre Poilievre, supported the convoy 100 per cent[215], and still does.[216]

We finally broke the fever of the pandemic restrictions. Until we came to Ottawa, there were only more restrictions planned, supposedly because of Omicron. But once we were there, provinces[217] suddenly began announcing they were ending their COVID mandates. Saskatchewan and Alberta announced they were ending vaccine passports and would start lifting mask requirements. Quebec announced it would be lifting most restrictions by March. Ontario, B.C. and Manitoba began announcing they would lift restrictions, too.

We transformed politics in Alberta. Jason Kenney was the premier during the Freedom Convoy. After his support for masking, vaccine passports and vaccine mandates, he was forced to resign due to lack of support from his party. In October, he was replaced by Danielle Smith. She has forcefully denounced the discrimination faced by unvaccinated people and has promised[218] there will be no more vaccine mandates,

---

214 https://nationalpost.com/news/canada/first-reading-did-the-truckers-get-erin-otoole-fired

215 https://nationalpost.com/opinion/pierre-poilievre-says-his-freedom-fight-includes-truckers-full-comment-with-anthony-furey

216 https://nationalpost.com/news/poilievre-freedom-convoy-protesters

217 https://globalnews.ca/news/8614698/quebec-weighs-suspending-covid-vaccine-passport/

218 https://www.westernstandard.news/alberta/ucp-leadership-candidate-danielle-smith-promises-no-more-lockdowns/article_890ff19a-f23b-11ec-b329-234cbf0ed720.html

no more vaccine passports, no more masking kids[219], and no more lockdowns in Alberta as long as she's premier.

And we shamed the federal government. The inquiry into their use of the Emergencies Act has been a huge embarrassment for the Trudeau Liberals. Every police official who testified was clear that they didn't need the Emergencies Act. That they had plenty of tools for managing a peaceful protest that didn't involve invoking the modern-day equivalent of the War Measures Act. Every single intelligence officer that testified blew apart the lies spread by Trudeau and his friends in the media that we were violent, foreign-funded extremists trying to overthrow the government.

The inquiry has seen evidence that when the Ontario deputy solicitor general suggested[220] letting Freedom Convoy leaders meet "provincial and federal ministers so that they could be heard in an attempt to de-escalate" the situation, Trudeau's people simply refused. Trudeau was completely against it, telling his colleagues we were an "armed insurrection"[221] that was "terrorizing" Canada.

All of Trudeau's militancy, his paranoia and his vanity has been exposed. Every single one of his lies has been exposed. The inquiry has proved beyond doubt that we were a grassroots movement of real Canadians who simply wanted to come to the nation's capital to be heard. And that Trudeau viciously made us his enemies and declared war on us because we had dared to speak truth to power.

But I think the biggest thing the Freedom Convoy exposed was the lie about Canada being a divided country.

Before this all happened, I had spent some time supporting the Alberta separatist movement. In 2019, I joined the boards of Wexit

---

219 https://calgaryherald.com/news/local-news/smith-vow-to-prevent-future-school-mask-mandates-draws-criticism

220 https://twitter.com/RebelNews_CA/status/1590821841656254464

221 https://www.theepochtimes.com/trudeau-feared-an-armed-insurrection-said-freedom-convoy-wouldnt-be-resolved-by-talking_4858338.html

Alberta and Wexit Canada, as well as the separatist Maverick Party. I had decided, like so many Albertans, that the rest of Canada didn't want Alberta, and so we shouldn't want the rest of Canada. At that point, Justin Trudeau had been elected twice on platforms that blatantly targeted Alberta and its energy industry and punished us just for being who we are.

I actually ended up quitting the Maverick Party when I was in Ottawa for the protest, after they told me they were not interested in standing up against vaccine mandates. In fact, a couple of the board members were actually pro-lockdown and pro-mandates.

In reality, my heart wasn't even in separatism anymore. I remember a few nights before we headed out to Ottawa, and I was sitting at my kitchen table helping to get things organized, and I was chatting with people from the West and Ontario, and on one screen I had a chat going with the Quebec group, and I was using Google Translate to help me. And it hit me that these people were just like us, they felt the same things as us. And then, when we travelled across this great country, and when we spent those weeks in Ottawa, I knew for a fact that it was true.

We have different cultures, different backgrounds, different languages. But I learned that we are all the same. We all want our freedoms. We all want futures for our children and our grandchildren.

Here in the West, all we've heard is Justin Trudeau attacking us for our way of life. And other politicians, like NDP Leader Jagmeet Singh, Bloc Québécois Leader Yves-Francois Blanchet and Elizabeth May's Green Party, calling for Ottawa to shut down our energy industry and put us all out of jobs. And all we hear from the news and from social media is how much Quebec hates us and Ontario hates us and how they don't want our dirty oil.

The Freedom Convoy made me realize this was all a big lie. People had come together from across Canada, from the clan mothers in the North to the truckers from the West, the East and everywhere in between. And the crowds that came to cheer us, those massive crowds, full of young and old, families and nuns, Native dancers and Hutterites; from the proud rednecks on their snowmobiles riding the shoulder with their hockey-stick Canadian flags to the Ottawa bureaucrats who brought us blankets and food. I saw that we are all the same nation, with the same pride for this wonderful country, and the same love of freedom.

We showed that Trudeau doesn't speak for Canada. The Freedom Convoy proved that we, the people, speak for Canada. We spoke more loudly to the world than Trudeau has ever done. We changed world history. We are not the racists he calls us. We are not the committers of genocide that he accuses us of being. We are not the phobics that he claims are everywhere. We are not a nation to be ashamed of, and Canadians have nothing to apologize for.

The values we share are bigger than petty and divisive politics. This nation was proud and strong and united for 148 years before Trudeau was elected, and I believe it will stay that way long after he's gone. The convoy proved that COVID couldn't domesticate us. It couldn't suppress our spirit of freedom. It proved that the government could not control us. We showed that we, and we alone, will determine our futures. And Trudeau, with his cowardly use of the Emergencies Act, will not stand in the way of the aspirations Canadians have for ourselves, our families and our nation.

I know now, with absolute certainty, that Canada is an incredible country and I love it deeply, with my heart and soul. The people of this country are truly strong and free. And I will devote whatever time God gives me on this earth to fighting back against those politicians and those in the media who want to divide and weaken us.

And I ask you to join me, because I know now that God has put me here to make the great nation of Canada stronger, freer and more united.

I've already started taking French lessons.

Printed in Great Britain
by Amazon

25049934R00126